THE FLORIDA SEAFOOD COOKBOOK

HOW TO BUY, CLEAN, PREPARE, AND COOK FLORIDA SEAFOOD

By J. Kent Thompson

Copyright © 2016 by J. Kent Thompson.

All rights reserved. No part of this book may be reproduced in any form or by any means, electronic or mechanical, including photocopying, recording, or by any information storage and retrieval system without permission in writing from the publisher.

ISBN 978-1-329-70467-1

Extra copies can be ordered @lulu.com/shop/

Contact the author @ jkt416@gmail.com

Cover photos by the author

1st Paperback Edition

INTRODUCTION

I have found that while everyone enjoys eating Florida seafood, not many know how to prepare it. In this cookbook I want to help you overcome any fears you may have on how to clean and/or cook fish and shellfish you have either caught or bought. It is really not that hard to prepare great seafood. In this book I give you just the basics. If you want to go further you will now have the confidence to take on the fancy dishes.

The recipes and diagrams contained in this book are not necessarily original but are compiled from the kitchens of the former Florida Board of Conservation, the Florida Department of Natural Resources, and include the personal favorites of me and my friends. Until this publication, many of these recipes had been lost to the ages.

I have enjoyed using these recipes over the years while serving as an officer with the Florida Marine Patrol, and the Florida Fish and Wildlife Conservation Commission. Now I have the privilege to share them with you.

This cookbook is dedicated to those who protect Florida's natural resources and the commercial fishermen who toil long hours to provide fresh, wild-caught Florida seafood for your table each day.

In no time you, the aspiring fisher/cook, will be preparing some of Florida's best seafood recipes. I hope you enjoy them! JKT

TABLE OF CONTENTS

THE BASICS:

1. *BUYING SEAFOOD* — page 11

2. *HOW TO CLEAN SEAFOOD FOR COOKING* — page 19

3. *METHODS OF COOKING SEAFOOD* — page 31

FAVORITE SEAFOOD RECIPES

4. *POACHED, STEAMED AND SIMMERED FISH* — page 45

5. *FRIED FISH* — page 41

6. *BAKED FISH* — page 43

7. *OVEN FRY FISH* — page 45

8. *BROILED FISH* — page 49

9. *SHRIMP* — page 51

10	*FLORIDA LOBSTER*	page 63
11	*BLUE CRABS*	page 69
12	*STONE CRABS*	page 75
13	*OYSTERS*	page 77
14	*SCALLOPS*	page 83
15	*SPREADS, DIPS, SAUCES, AND SIDES*	page 89

CHAPTER ONE—THE BASICS: BUYING SEAFOOD

DIFFERENT FORMS OF FISH YOU WILL SEE IN THE DISPLAY CASE

WHOLE OR ROUND FISH: are sold just as they come from the water. Before they are cooked they must be eviscerated (have the entrails removed) and scaled. Usually the head, fins, and tail are also removed.

DRAWN FISH: have had the entrails removed. Before they are cooked the fish must be scaled, and the head, fins, and tail are usually removed.

DRESSED OR PAN-DRESSED FISH: are scaled and eviscerated and may be cooked in this form. The smaller the fish, weighing one pound or less, called pan-dressed, sometimes have the heads and tails left on. Larger, dressed fish usually have the heads removed.

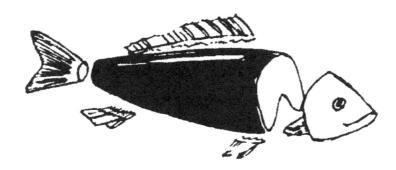

STEAKS: are made by cutting a large dressed fish across the backbone at intervals of 5/8 inches to 1 ¾ inches. Steaks are ready to cook.

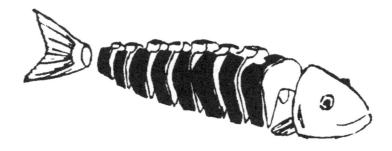

FILLETS: are the sides of dressed fish, cut lengthwise away from the backbone. Fillets are practically boneless and are ready to cook.

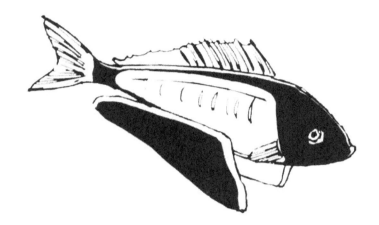

BUTTERFLY FILLETS: are the two sides or fillets of fish held together by the uncut belly skin. This is a popular form for outdoor cooking. To keep the form intact during cooking, the bones and scales are sometimes left on the fish.

HOW TO DETERMINE FRESHNESS

FOR FRESH FISH:

Look for the following signs of freshness when buying fresh whole or drawn fish;

Eyes- are they bright, clear and bulging?

Gills- are they bright red in color and free of slime?

Scales- do they adhere tightly to the skin?

Flesh- is it firm and elastic?

Does exposed flesh appear fresh-cut with no traces of browning or drying out?
Colors of skin- are the iridescent and un-faded characteristic markings and colors of that species evident?

Smell- should be fresh and mild odor, with no disagreeable "fishy odor".

FOR DRESSED FISH, FILLETS OR STEAKS:

They should be fresh cut in appearance without traces of browning around the edges.

They should not have a dried out appearance on the surface.

They should have firm, elastic flesh with a mild, fresh odor.

FOR FROZEN FISH:

Good quality frozen fish have these characteristics;

Frozen fish should be solidly frozen.

Flesh- Is solidly frozen with no discoloration in the flesh. Check for freezer burn, (a very white, dry appearance around the edges, also examine the package for ice crystals which may form around the inside of the package or be concentrated in one area of the package). Both of these are signs that indicate moisture loss from the fish flesh and could be the result of thawing and refreezing.

Wrapping- Fish is wrapped in moisture-vapor proof materials with little or no air-space between the fish and the wrapping. The quality of the fish wrapped in plastic is generally better if the plastic is vacuum-packed rather than over-wrapped.
Packages of frozen fish should be kept below the freezer line in open freezer cases.

If frozen fish is over wrapped in clear wrap, examine the fish for freezer burn (an uneven dry, white appearance on the skin that indicates moisture loss and flavor loss).

Odor- Frozen fish of good quality have little or no odor.

HOW MUCH DO I NEED TO BUY?

As a general rule, allow about one pound per person when you buy whole or drawn fish and about ½ pound per person when buying dressed fish. For steaks and fillets, allow about 1/3 pound per person or 2 pounds for 6 people. For the purpose of cooking and freezing instructions, fish are loosely grouped into two categories- **fat** and **lean**, based on the type and amount of oil and the flavor of the fish. Although the groupings are generally accepted, the amount of oil will vary according to the time of year, and some of the fish fluctuate from fat to lean.

"LEAN FISH"

"Lean fish" is a designation given to fish species with a fat content from 0.5 percent to not more than five percent, with the oil in some of these fish characteristically concentrated in the liver. Some common Florida species in this category are: **Weakfish or Sea Trout, Black Sea Bass, Sheephead, Grouper, Black and Red Drum, flounder, Snapper (Lane, Mangrove, Mutton, Red, Vermilion,**

Yellowtail) Whiting, Scamp, Shark, Tilefish, Triggerfish, and Warsaw.

Due to low oil content, these fish maintain quality during freezing up to six months and the very leanest can be held in the freezer up to a year.

"FAT FISH"

"Fat fish" is a general name given to fish which have an oil content of more than five percent. Since the oil is distributed throughout the flesh of the fish, the flesh color of the fat fish tends to be darker than that of a leaner species. The exact percentage of oil in the fish flesh depends on such variables as species, season of the year, and even the water depth from which the fish is taken. Some common Florida species in this category are: **Spanish Mackerel, King Mackerel, Mullet (Black and Silver), Permit, Porgy, Bluefish, Amberjack, Eel, Croaker, Spot, Swordfish and Pompano.**

These fish do not freeze as well as lean fish and it is recommended that they be used within three months.

KEEP THESE GENERAL HINTS IN MIND WHEN SELECTING A FISH FOR RECIPE PREPARATION:

1. As a general rule, the species which contain higher percentages of oil have <u>more flavors</u>. Lean fish may be substituted for fat fish in a recipe, but the flavor of the fish may be masked and more frequent basting may be required due to the lower oil content.

2. If a recipe preparation requires frequent handling of the fish, as in chowders, soups or pickling, a firm-textured fish (grouper, red drum and tilefish) will retain its shape and have a more pleasing finished appearance.

3. Cooking time will vary according to the thickness and the size of the fish. To prevent overcooking, the fish should be tested about halfway through the recommended cooking time and frequently thereafter until the fish flakes easily when tested with a fork.

HOW SOON DO I HAVE TO USE THE FISH AFTER I BUY THEM?

Plan to use fresh fish within two days of catch/purchase. If unable to use it in two days, then cook it. Cooked fish maintains quality in the refrigerator for two to three days if stored in the coolest part of the refrigerator. Maximum quality in fresh fish is maintained if fish is kept in the refrigerator and loosely wrapped and packed in finely crushed ice to prevent moisture loss. Handle seafood with care by making it the last purchase on a trip to the store. Take fish home immediately and place them in the refrigerator or freezer.

FREEZING AND THAWING FRESH FISH

You may freeze fish at home in a block of ice or by glazing, both methods prevent moisture loss. To freeze fresh bought or caught fish (or shrimp) in a solid block of ice, place them in a container and fill with water. They should be completely covered by the water. Place in the freezer until solidly frozen.

HOW TO GLAZE FISH

Glazing is as effective as block freezing and takes up less space in the freezer. To glaze the fish, you may dress and steak, or fillet it if desired. Place fish in a single layer on a tray, wrap and freeze. As soon as the fish is solidly frozen, remove from freezer, unwrap and dip it quickly into ice cold water; a glaze will form immediately. Repeat the dipping three or four times. A thin coat of ice will result from each dipping. It may be necessary to return fish to the freezer between dipping if glaze does not continue to build up. Handle the fish carefully to avoid breaking the glaze. Wrap the fish tightly in freezer paper or aluminum foil and return to the freezer. Glazing may need to be repeated if fish are not used within one to two months.

THAWING FISH

Thaw frozen fish by placing in the refrigerator, allowing 18 to 24 hours for a one-pound package to thaw. For a quicker method of thawing, whole or drawn fish may be placed under cold running water.

Fillets, steaks and dressed fish may be cooked as if they were thawed but you need to allow a little extra cooking time.

NEVER thaw at room temperature and NEVER refreeze.

CHAPTER TWO

HOW TO CLEAN SEAFOOD FOR COOKING

HOW TO DRESS A WHOLE OR ROUND FISH

1. Lay the fish on a board and grasp the head firmly.
2. Using a fish scaler or a large tablespoon, scrape the scales off, working from the tail to the head.
3. Make a cut the entire length of the belly and remove the entrails and the pelvic fins.
4. Using a sharp knife, remove the head and the pectoral fins by making a cut just in front of the collarbone. If the backbone is large, cut down to it on either side and snap the head off.
5. Remove the dorsal fin by cutting along each side with a sharp knife and grasp the end near the tail with one hand and give a quick pull toward the head.
6. Clean and rinse the fish thoroughly.
7. The fish is now *dressed*, or *pan-dressed*.
8. With one additional step a large dressed fish can be *steaked* by cutting across the backbone with a sharp knife at approximately 1 to 1 ¼ inch intervals.

(SEE DIAGRAM ON PAGE 20)

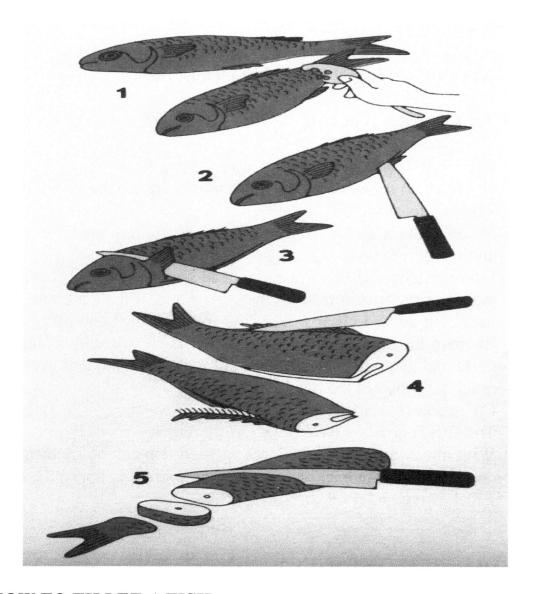

HOW TO FILLET A FISH

If you want to fillet your fish, it is not necessary to completely dress the fish.

1. Scale the fish, (unless the fillet is to be skinned).
2. With a sharp knife, cut through the flesh along the backbone from the tail to just behind the head.
3. Cut down to the backbone just behind the collarbone.

4. Turn the knife flat and slide along the rib bones to the tail, cutting the flesh away from the backbone. Turn the fish over and repeat the process.

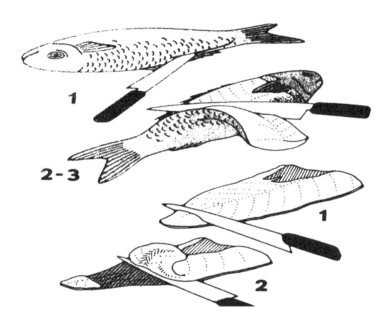

HOW TO SKIN A FISH

(This is easier to do when the fillet has not been scaled.)

1. Lay the fillet, skin side down, on a cutting board. Hold the tail end of the fillet with the fingers of one hand. With a sharp knife at an angle, make a cut about ½-inch from the fingers through the flesh to the skin, being careful not to cut through the skin.

2. Lay the knife blade flat against the skin and push the knife forward along the skin while holding the free end of the skin firmly with the fingers.

HOW TO CLEAN SHRIMP

The cleaning method for shrimp is the same whether raw or cooked, but it is easier when the shrimp is raw. I would recommend you invest in a shrimp peeling/de-veining tool. There are several varieties of shrimp peeling and de-veining tools on the market. Some work better than others but all are designed, when properly used, to quickly and easily remove the shell and vein from the shrimp in one easy motion.

Shrimp peeling / de-veining tool

If a cleaning tool is not available, it can be done by hand in the following method;

To peel: hold the tail of the shrimp in one hand; slip the thumb of other hand under the shell between the swimmeret's and lift off several segments of shell. Repeat the process, if necessary, removing all but the tail section.

If tail section is to be removed: hold the tail section and squeeze with the thumb and forefinger. Pull the shrimp meat with the other hand until it is released from the shell.

The vein: (usually black) located along the upper curve is commonly referred to as the "sand vein". The vein is part of the circulatory system and need not be removed. I would recommend removing it to eliminate sand or grit in the cooked shrimp. It can be removed before or after cooking but is easier to remove before the shrimp is cooked.

To remove the vein, make a cut with a sharp knife about 1/8-inch-deep along the upper curve of the shrimp; then rinse away the sand vein under cold running water.

HOW TO CLEAN A BLUE CRAB

1. With crab upside down, grasp legs on one side firmly with one hand, and with the other hand lift the flap (apron) and pull back and down to remove the top shell.

2. Turn the crab right side up, remove the gills and wash out the intestines and spongy material.

3. With a twisting motion pull the legs loose from the body. Remove any meat which adheres to the legs. Break off claws.

4. Slice off the top of the inner skeleton and remove all exposed meat on this slice. At the back of the crab, on each side, lies a large lump of meat. With a very careful U-shaped motion of the knife, remove this back fin lump.

5. Remove the white flake meat from the other pockets with the point of the knife.

6. Crack the claw shell and remove the shell along the movable pincer. This will expose the claw meat and, if meat is left attached to the remaining pincer, will make a delicious (crab finger) hors d'oeuvre. Or the dark meat can be removed and used in soups, casseroles or salads.

(SEE DIAGRAM ON PAGE 24)

HOW TO CLEAN A BLUE CRAB

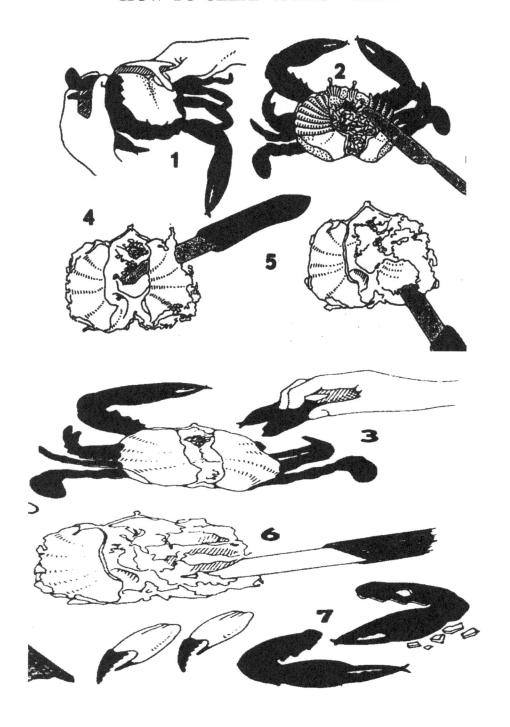

24

HOW TO CLEAN A FLORIDA LOBSTER

Cleaning boiled lobster and preparing green lobster for baking are the same; lay lobster on its back, with a sharp knife cut lobster in half lengthwise remove stomach which in the body section and intestinal vein which runs from the stomach to the tip of the tail. Rinse and clean body cavity thoroughly. The green lobster is ready for baking. If lobster is boiled and the meat needs to be removed from the shell use a sharp knife to loosen the meat from the edges of the shell. With a fork, pierce the meat at the tip of the tail and lift upward and pull the meat toward the head away from the shell.

HOW TO SHUCK AN OYSTER

First you need good gloves (cotton or rubberized) and an oyster knife. An oyster knife is a heavy piece of metal with a wedge shaped blade and handle in one piece, designed to withstand the pressure required to open oysters. Don't try to open oysters with only your bare hands and a sharp knife or oyster knife—I guarantee if you do, someone—you—are going to get hurt. Rinse the oyster thoroughly. The cleanest way to open oysters is to grasp the oyster securely by the thin end or "bill" leaving the hinge (thicker portion) exposed towards the other hand. Usually there is a small crevice at the hinge.

1. Insert the oyster knife in this crevice between the shells; twist the knife while pushing it firmly into the opening to sever the hinge.
2. Once the hinge is broken, before pulling the shell apart slide the knife along the inside of the top shell and cut the adductor muscle loose from the shell.
3. Remove the top shell and again slip the knife under the oyster being careful not to mutilate the oyster, and cut the muscle away from the bottom shell. Remove any remaining shell particles which may be attached to the oyster. Most oysters, except for the largest, can be opened by this method. For larger oysters, another method is to break apart the shell on the thin end with a hammer to make an opening. Insert the knife in the opening and slide along the inside of top shell to cut the adductor muscle and then cut oyster away from remaining shell. This method tends to leave more shell particles on the oyster. Be careful not to mutilate the oyster.

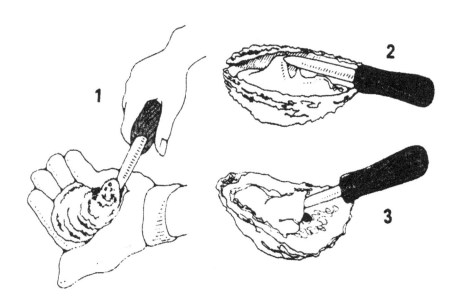

SERVING STONE CRAB CLAWS

This is a treat in itself where everyone can get involved;

1. Place the claw in a kitchen towel before cracking to catch any bits of shell or juices from inside the shell then crack all the sections of shell with a hammer or nutcracker.
2. Let hungry guests pick out the meat for themselves.

The claw portion also makes an attractive hors d'oeuvre or appetizer, to serve crack the claw and remove the shell and movable pincer leaving the meat attached to the remaining pincer. The cooked meat can also be picked from the shell and used in any recipe calling for cooked crabmeat or lobster. Approximately 2 ½ pounds of cooked stone crab claws are required to yield one pound of crabmeat

HOW TO CLEAN/SHUCK A SCALLOP

Hold the scallop in the palm of one hand with the shells hinge against the palm.

1. Insert a slender strong knife, not sharp (a dinner knife will do) or a spoon with the edge sharpened, between the halves of the shell near the hinge, then twist to give access to the inside. Do not force the shell open as this will tear the scallop muscle.
2. Lift the top side of the shell far enough to insert the knife point and sever the muscle from the top shell or with the spoon scrape the top inside of the shell to cut the muscle. Leave the muscle attached to the bottom shell until all viscera is removed.
3. To remove the viscera grip the dark portion of the scallop firmly between the thumb and knife blade or spoon and pull gently. This should remove everything but the edible white scallop muscle.

Another trick that works is after cutting loose the scallop from the top shell is to use a shop vacuum to suck the viscera away from the meat. After cleaning all your scallops, empty the vacuum canister and wash out thoroughly with Clorox.

4. When all viscera is removed, cut the muscle from the remaining shell and wash thoroughly in cold water, place in zip lock bag and ice.

I recommend you clean your catch while still on the water if recreationally harvesting, making sure you keep within the bag limit. It is a lot easier to do and saves on having to dispose of the shells and viscera at home.

(SEE DIAGRAM ON PAGE 29)

HOW TO CLEAN/SHUCK A SCALLOP

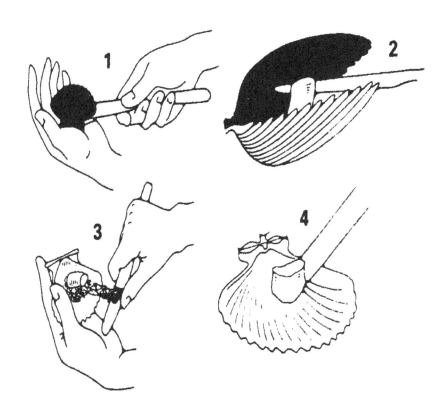

CHAPTER THREE

TEN METHODS OF COOKING SEAFOOD

There are many ways to cook seafood, each yielding its own flavorful delight. I suggest you try them all. In the chapters that follow I will provide you recipes using each method for the different types of seafood.

POACHING

Poaching is a low calorie way to prepare seafood for recipes that call for cooked, flaked fish. The food is cooked in a small amount of hot liquid, taking care to retain the shape of the food. Poached fish is simple and elegant to serve plain or with a sauce.

Poaching is a method of cooking which gives prominence to the flavor of the fish. Therefore, lean fish are generally preferred for this method of cooking. Fat fish are good poached if the fish is very fresh and a stronger flavored sauce is used to complement the more robust flavored fish. Many people who do poach fat fish remove not only the skin, but the wedge of dark flesh (usually reddish in color) where the oil is concentrated on both sides of a fish steak or down the center next to the skin on a fillet. Another way to prepare cooked, flaked fish is steaming.

STEAMING

To steam fish, place raw fish on a rack with openings, lower rack into kettle or steamer containing a small amount of boiling water and cover kettle tightly. Water level must be low enough so that only the steam produced from the boiling water cooks the fish.

SIMMERING

Simmering is cooking seafood in a liquid just below the boiling point, at a temperature of 185 degrees to 210 degrees. Bubbles should form slowly and collapse below the surface.
Simmering is the simplest method for preparing cooked, flaked fish. Fish can be also be simmered in a soup or chowder.

FRYING

Frying is a favorite way of preparing seafood in Florida, from the Keys to Pensacola it is the true Floridian's preferred way to cook fish and shrimp. Some people prefer pan-frying and others prefer deep frying. Both methods cook the food in oil. I recommend that you use peanut oil to fry your fish as it cooks cleaner and hotter. Pan frying or sautéing uses a small amount of oil while deep-frying requires a 3 to 4-inch depth of oil in which the food can be submerged. Allow room in your pot for bubbling oil to expand 40% or more.

CHOOSING AN OIL FOR FRYING

You can use any type of oil you prefer. The main thing is to choose one that will withstand high temperatures without burning. Canola Oil is low in cholesterol, withstands high heat without breaking down and has little flavor. Olive oil is good healthful oil and has the best flavor for simple fried foods, but is an expensive choice. I would recommend it for pan frying instead of deep frying. Corn oil can withstand high temperatures, is flavorful, but a little higher in cholesterol. I personally prefer to use Peanut oil, it burns hotter and cleaner and has little flavor.

OVEN FRYING

Oven-frying is baking fish, uncovered, at a very high temperature, 400 degrees to 500 degrees for a short period. The fish is breaded or coated in a mixture which, when cooked at this high temperature, will become crisp while preventing the fish from drying out during cooking

BAKING

Baking simply defined is to cook covered or uncovered in an oven or an oven type appliance. The temperature for baking seafood can vary from a warm 150 degrees to about 400 degrees. When fish is breaded and baked at higher temperatures (400 degrees to 500 degrees), the method of cooking is generally referred as oven frying.

BROILING

Broiling is cooking by direct heat, usually from above the food. Food is generally placed 3 to 4 inches from source of heat and basted with a sauce containing fat which prevents drying of the food. The food can also be dipped in an oily mixture before broiling. Lean fish require more basting than fat fish which contain natural oil to prevent them from drying out. Foods generally require one turning during broiling unless the food being broiled is very thin.

GRILLING

Grilling is cooking with a direct heat source from below the food. Food is placed on a rack 4 to 6 inches from the source of heat and basted with melted margarine, cooking oil or a sauce to keep from drying.

You can grill with charcoal, gas or electric. If using charcoal, line the fire bowl with heavy aluminum foil and stack the briquettes in a pyramid, if self lighting all you need to do is light, if regular briquettes, soak lightly with charcoal lighter fluid, let stand for one minute then light. Make sure your grill is in an open area with no overhangs that may catch fire or melt from the flames. Never use gasoline to start a fire. When the charcoal briquette is covered with a gray ash the fire is ready. Spread the coals out evenly so they are slightly wider than the cooking surface to be used. Wet wood chips can be added to create a smoke flavor to the items cooked if desired.

ROASTING

Roasting is cooking uncovered in hot air, and when used as a method of cooking seafood, is usually done outside around a fire or hot coals.

SMOKING

Smoking is slow cooking in a hooded or covered wood, charcoal, electric or gas grill. The heat must be kept low. Wet wood chips are used to create smoke, lower temperatures, and add flavor to the fish. Some smokers also use water bowls placed between the fire and the food being cooked to reduce heat and maintain moisture.

Temperatures can range from a low 150 to 175 degrees, which can give the fish a stronger smoke flavor, up to higher temperatures as much as 300 degrees. Cooking times will vary according to type of equipment used, the heat of the fire and the distance the seafood is from the source of heat.

Hardwood chips from hickory, cherry, apple oak or mesquite provide excellent smoke flavor to fish. Soak at least one pound of hardwood chips in 2 quarts of water for several hours or overnight before cooking.

CHAPTER FOUR—POACHED, STEAMED, AND SIMMERED FISH RECIPES

Use poaching, steaming, or simmering methods to prepare cooked, flaked fish in any of these delightful recipes. Leftover baked or fried fish from which the outer coating has been removed can be flaked and used in recipes calling for cooked, flaked fish. There are many recipes developed for cooked, flaked fish which provide versatility, economy, and eating enjoyment.

Poached fish

2 pounds of fish steaks or fillets, fresh or frozen (lean fish preferred)
2 cups water
¼ cup lemon juice
1 small onion
1 teaspoon salt
3 peppercorns
2 sprigs parsley
1 bay leaf
Hollandaise of fluffy lemon sauce* (see Chapter 15)
Paprika

Thaw fish if frozen. Remove skin from steaks and both skin and bones from fillets. Cut fish into serving size portions. Combine water, lemon juice, onion, salt, peppercorns, parsley and bay leaf in a well-greased 10-inch fry pan and bring to a boil. Reduce heat. Place fish in a single layer into the hot liquid. Cover and simmer 8 to 10 minutes or until fish flakes easily when tested with a fork. Carefully remove fish to a hot platter. Serve, if desired, with Hollandaise or Fluffy Lemon Sauce, or substitute a favorite sauce recipe. Sprinkle with paprika. Makes six servings.

There are many good sauces which may be served with hot or cold poached fish. Commercially packaged sauces are quick and easy and offer a wide selection, several which would complement poached fish. Fluffy Lemon Sauce and Hollandaise Sauce are two great sauces which may be served warm on hot poached fish. Prepare a Hollandaise sauce from any recipe, or follow directions on a commercially packaged sauce to whip up a delicious hollandaise sauce. Regardless of preparation methods, hollandaise sauce is excellent served warm over poached fish.

GULF FISH SALAD

2 ½ cups cooked, flaked fat or lean fish
2 cups cold cooked rice
1 cup chopped celery
½ cup chopped parsley
¼ cup sliced, pitted ripe olives
½ cup mayonnaise or salad dressing
2 tablespoons French dressing
2 tablespoons lemon juice
1 teaspoon curry powder
Salad greens

Combine fish, rice, celery, parsley and olives. Combine mayonnaise, French dressing, lemon juice and curry powder; mix thoroughly. Add mayonnaise to fish mixture and toss lightly. Chill. Serve on salad greens. Makes 6 servings.

FISH AND SPAGHETTI CASSEROLE

2 cups cooked, flaked fat or lean fish
½ cup (4 ounces) of mushrooms
2 tablespoons all purpose flour
1 teaspoon salt
¼ teaspoon pepper
2 tablespoons melted butter
1¼ cup milk
1 cup grated cheddar cheese
2 tablespoons chopped pimiento
2 cups cooked spaghetti
1 cup dry bread crumbs
2 tablespoons melted butter

Drain mushrooms, reserving liquid. Blend flour and seasonings into butter. Add milk cook until thick and smooth, stirring constantly. Add cheese, pimiento, mushrooms, and fish; stir until well blended. Layer half of the spaghetti, and then half the fish mixture in a well greased 1 ½ quart casserole. Repeat layers. Combine crumbs and butter; sprinkle over top of casserole. Bake in a moderate oven, 350 degrees, for 15 to 20 minutes or until bubbly. Makes 6 servings.

SIMMERED FISH

To prepare approximately 2 cups of cooked, flaked fish, place 1 ½ pounds fat or lean fish fillets in 1 quart boiling water, salted with 1 tablespoon salt. Cover and reduce heat. Simmer for 8 to 10 minutes or until fish flakes easily when tested with a fork. Drain. Remove skin and bones. Flake by breaking the fish into small, medium or large pieces, according to the specifications of the recipe in which it is to be used.

SEA GARDEN CHOWDER

1 pound fat or lean fish fillets (fresh or frozen)
½ cup chopped onion
2 tablespoons melted butter
2 cups diced potatoes
1 cup boiling water
¾ teaspoon salt
Pepper to season
2 cups milk
1 cup (8 ounces) cream corn
Chopped parsley (garnish)

Thaw fish if frozen. Skin fillets and cut the fillets into pieces about 1 inch square. In a 3-quart saucepan, cook onion in butter until tender, but not brown. Add potatoes, water, salt and pepper. Cover and simmer for 10 minutes. Add fish and simmer 5 to 10 minutes longer or until fish flakes easily when tested with a fork and potatoes are tender. Add the milk and cream corn. Heat but do not boil. Serve hot. Garnish with parsley. Makes 6 servings.

SHIRLEY'S CALLALOU (FISH SOUP)

3 tablespoons butter
½ cup chopped onion
Sauté onion then add ½ lb. fresh spinach cut into strips, cook until limp
Add 3 cups chicken broth and ½ cup coconut milk
Simmer 10 minutes
Salt and pepper to taste.
Add ½ lb. fish cut into small pieces.
Cook until done-3 to 5 minutes
Add 1½ cups milk and heat until hot

A crowd pleaser! (Coconut milk is available in the can at your local store. You may also add fresh sliced mushrooms to the onion's when you sauté if desired.)

CHAPTER FIVE---- FRIED FISH

The real secret to being successful when you fry fish is to be prepared. You want to be able to have your fish go from the fryer to the plate as quickly as possible to maximize flavor. Have the table set, all of your ingredients prepared, any sauces made, and any side dishes ready. I have included three recipes for side dishes that accompany fried fish (or any seafood for that matter) they are hushpuppies, cheese grits, and coleslaw. They can be found in the Spreads. Dip, Sauces, and Sides recipe's in chapter 15.

TO PAN-FRY

Place fish in a heavy fry pan which contains about 1/8 inch of oil, hot but not smoking. Fry at moderate heat, 360 degrees, for 4 to 5 minutes or until brown. Turn carefully and cook 4 to 5 minutes longer or until brown and fish flakes easily when tested with a fork. Remove from oil and drain on paper towels. Serve with a sauce if desired. Makes 6 servings.

TO DEEP-FRY

Place fish in a deep-fry basket and cook in hot oil 3 to 4 inches deep at 350 degrees for 2 to 3 minutes. Turn fish once when crisp and golden brown. If frying fillets, brown the skin side last. Remove from oil and drain on paper towels. Makes 6 servings.

Florida Golden Brown Fried Fish

2 pounds fat or lean fish (fresh or frozen)
2/3 cup cornmeal*
½ teaspoon salt
½ teaspoon paprika
Oil for frying

Thaw fish if frozen. Skin the fillets. Cut fillets into serving size portions. Combine cornmeal, salt and paprika. Roll fish in cornmeal mixture or put in a paper or plastic bag and shake until fish are covered with meal mixture)

* For finer texture, use 1/3 cup corn meal mixed with 1/3 cup all purpose flour. I use Alabama Fine Grind or Hoover's brand, but any available cornmeal will do.

Regardless of the method you use, Florida Golden Brown Fried Fish is great to eat either with or without a sauce. You can even just dip it in ketchup if that's your style. Two sauces that you may want to try are tartar or sweet and sour sauce (see chapter 15).

CHAPTER SIX---BAKED FISH

Seafood can be baked with or without a sauce, without a topping or in a casserole, stuffed or very basic. Here are recipes for basic Florida Baked Fish and several other variations of baked fish.

Florida Basic Baked Fish

3 or 4 pounds dressed fish (fresh or frozen), lean fish preferred
1 ½ teaspoons salt
½ teaspoon pepper
2 tablespoons melted butter

Thaw fish if frozen. Clean, wash and dry the fish. Sprinkle inside and outside with salt and pepper. Place fish on a well greased bake-and-serve- platter. Brush with oil and baste occasionally during cooking. Bake in a moderate oven, 350 degrees, for 30 to 40 minutes or until fish flakes easily when tested with a fork. Makes 6 servings.

2 pound fillets may be prepared by this method, but seasonings should be reduced to 1 teaspoon salt and ¼ teaspoon pepper. Cooking time for fillets should be reduced to 15 to 20 minutes or until fish flakes easily when tested with a fork.

Florida Basic Baked Fish may be served in several ways. Either Hollandaise or Fluffy Lemon Sauce (Fluffy Lemon Sauce recipe is in Ch. 15), will complement the baked fish. Or add ½ cup (4 ounces) sliced mushrooms to one package of (1 ounce) white wine sauce mix, prepared according to package directions and pour over baked fish.

Both the dressed fish and fish fillets can be stuffed. The cavity of dressed fish should be stuffed loosely and closed with small skewers or toothpicks, and laced with string. Bake according to Florida Basic Baked Fish directions and remove skewers and string before serving.

If fillets are stuffed, place stuffing on top of one fillet, cover with another fillet of the same size and bake according to fillet instructions.

Orange-Rice Stuffing is one suggestion. Another appears in the Blue Crab Section and makes an excellent stuffing for flounder.

ORANGE-RICE STUFFING

1 cup chopped celery with leaves
¼ cup chopped onion
¼ cup melted butter
¼ cup diced. Sectioned, pared oranges
2 tablespoons lemon juice
1 tablespoon grated orange rind
¾ teaspoon salt
1 cup cooked white rice
½ cup toasted, blanched, slivered almonds

Cook celery and onion in butter until tender. Combine all ingredients; mix thoroughly. Makes 3 cups stuffing.

Fish can be baked, stuffed or baked in a sauce or with a breading. Baking fish offers much versatility. You can bread your fish with one of the commercial breading mixtures for fish available at the store, and bake according to package directions. Or bake fish in a sauce by placing 2 pounds fat or lean fish seasoned with ½ teaspoon salt in a baking dish. Pour 1 package (1 ounce) white wine sauce mix, prepared according to package directions, over fish. Sprinkle with paprika and bake at 350 degrees, for 15 to 20 minutes or until fish flakes easily when tested with a fork. Spanish Mackerel is great prepared this way!

CHAPTER SEVEN---OVEN FRY FISH

The following recipes are variations of coatings which can be used for oven-frying.

Florida Basic Oven-Fried Fish

2 pounds' fat or lean fish fillets or steaks (fresh or frozen), lean fish preferred
½ cup evaporated milk
1 teaspoon salt
1 ½ cups corn flake crumbs
¼ cup cooking oil

Thaw fish if frozen. Cut fish into serving-sized portions. Combine milk and salt. Dip fish in milk and roll in crumbs. Place fish in a single layer, skin side down, on a well greased baking pan, 15x10x1 inches. Drizzle oil over fish. Bake in an extremely hot oven, 500 degrees, for 10 to 12 minutes or until fish flakes easily when tested with a fork. Makes 6 servings.

FISHERMAN'S PREFERENCE

2 pounds fat fish fillets (fresh or frozen)
½ cup cooking oil
1 teaspoon salt
Dash pepper
1 clove garlic, minced
1 cup shredded cheddar cheese
1 cup fine corn flake or cracker crumbs
1 cup barbecue sauce

Thaw fish if frozen. Dry fillets. Cut into serving-size portions. Combine oil, salt, pepper and garlic. Mix cheese and crumbs. Dip fish in oil mixture and roll in crumb mixture. Place fish on a well greased baking pan. Bake in a very hot oven, 450 degrees, for 6 to 8 minutes. Heat barbecue sauce. Spoon half of sauce over fish. Cook fish an additional 3 to 5 minutes or until fish flakes easily when tested with a fork. Serve with remaining warm barbecue sauce. Makes 6 servings. Plan to have leftovers when preparing Fisherman's Preference and save time by serving leftovers in a bun with a little warm barbecue sauce poured over the fish. It's sure to be a hit the second time around as well!

Atlantic Coast Baked Steaks combine two methods of cooking; pan-frying and baking. The fish steaks should be fried as quickly as possible just to brown the surface, and then cooked internally during baking.

ATLANTIC COAST BAKED STEAKS

** King Mackerel steaks are excellent in this recipe.

2 pounds fat fish steaks, 1 to 1 ¼ inch thick (fresh or frozen)
1 teaspoon salt
¼ teaspoon pepper
¼ cup all-purpose flour
Fat for frying
1 ½ cups diced, seeded, peeled tomatoes
1 cup fresh sliced mushrooms
¼ cup dry vermouth
¼ teaspoon crushed garlic
½ cup soft bread crumbs
2 tablespoons melted butter

Thaw fish if frozen. Sprinkle steaks with salt and pepper and roll in flour. Place steaks in a single layer in a 12-inch fry pan containing 1/8 inch of fat, hot but not smoking. Fry quickly at high heat, 375 degrees for 3 to 4 minutes to brown steaks on both sides, turning carefully.

Place steaks in a single layer in a well greased baking dish 12x8x2 inches. In a one-quart saucepan, combine tomatoes, mushrooms, vermouth and garlic. Bring to a boil, stirring constantly. Pour hot sauce over fish. Combine bread crumbs and butter. Sprinkle crumbs over top of fish. Bake in a moderate oven, 350 degrees, for 15 to 20 minutes or until fish flakes easily when tested with a fork and crumbs are golden brown. Makes 6 servings.

CHAPTER EIGHT—BROILED FISH

Florida Basic Broiled Fish

2 pounds fat or lean fish fillets or steaks, fresh or frozen
2 tablespoons melted butter
2 tablespoons lemon juice
1 teaspoon salt
½ teaspoon paprika
Dash pepper

Thaw fish if frozen. Cut fillets into serving-size portions. Place fish in a single layer, skin side up, on a well greased baking pan, 15x 10x1 inches. Combine remaining ingredients and mix well. Pour sauce over fish. Broil about 4 inches from source of heat for 4 to 6 minutes. Turn carefully and baste with sauce. Broil 4 to 6 minutes longer or until fish flakes easily when tested with a fork. Makes 6 servings.

On the following pages are two other, quick and easy ways to broil fish, one for "fat fish" and one for "lean".

SHELLFISH COMMMISSIONER TEXAS "RUFF" HODGES FAVORITE

2 pounds fat fish fillets (fresh or frozen)
1 teaspoon salt
¼ teaspoon pepper
½ cup salad dressing or mayonnaise
2 tablespoons ketchup
2 tablespoons prepared mustard

Thaw fish if frozen. Cut fillets into serving-size portions. Sprinkle fillets with salt and pepper. Place fish, skin side down, on a well greased bake-and-serve platter. Broil fillets approximately 4 inches from source of heat for 10 minutes. Combine salad dressing, ketchup and mustard. Spread mixture evenly over fillets. Broil 4 to 5 minutes longer or until sauce bubbles and is lightly browned. Makes 6 servings.

CAPTAIN DUCKWORTH'S FAVORITE

2 pounds lean fish fillets (fresh or frozen)
2 tablespoons butter, softened
2 teaspoons chopped parsley
2 teaspoons grated lemon rind
½ cup Italian dressing
½ teaspoon salt
Dash pepper
1 cup dry bread crumbs
Lemon wedges, parsley (garnish)

Thaw fish if frozen. Skin fillets and cut into serving-size portions. Cream butter, parsley, and lemon rind; chill. Combine salad dressing, salt and pepper and mix thoroughly. Dip fish in dressing and roll in crumbs. Place fish on a well greased bake-and-serve platter, 15x10x1 inches. Broil about 3 inches from source of heat for 4 to 6 minutes. Turn carefully. Broil 4 to 6 minutes longer or until fish flakes easily when tested with a fork. Top each serving with approximately 1 teaspoon lemon-parsley butter. Garnish with lemon wedges and parsley. Makes 6 servings.

There are many types of sauces that can be used for basting fish during broiling. Use approximately ¾ cup of your favorite sauce, a commercial salad dressing, or try the Spicy BastingSauce recipe found in chapter 15 to baste fat or lean fish during broiling. Use the same cooking procedure as for Florida Basic Broiled Fish.

CHAPTER NINE--SHRIMP

Shrimp is one of the most popular shellfish in the United States. They have a distinctive flavor, and the pink-white cooked meat is tender, delicate and delicious. Shrimp may be prepared in hundreds of ways and served for almost any course in a menu. Shrimp are an excellent source for high quality protein, vitamins and minerals and because they are low in calories and easy to digest, they can fit into many special diets.

The shrimp is a ten legged crustacean that wears its skeleton on the outside. Shrimp from the warm waters of the Gulf and Atlantic grow larger than their cold water cousins. The species of warm water shrimp most commonly found in the market are white, brown, pink and rock shrimp. Any variety can be used in a shrimp recipe.

"GREEN" SHRIMP:

A term used to describe raw shrimp of any species in the shell. Regardless of the color, when cooked the shells of all species will turn red, the meat will become white with reddish tinges and the flavor and nutritional values will be the same.

BUYING SHRIMP BY "COUNT"

Shrimp are usually sold according to the size or grade based on the number of headless shrimp per pound. This is indicated with the names jumbo, large medium and small with jumbo indicating 20 or less shrimp per pound, and small 40 or more per pound. When buying shrimp, you will hear it said that the shrimp are 30-35 count or 50-60 count, each refers to the amount of shrimp it takes to make a pound and indicates the size of the shrimp. A 30-35 count means you are going to get a good sized shrimp while a 50-60 count would indicate small "popcorn" shrimp.

DETERMINING FRESHNESS

Fresh shrimp are firm in texture and have a mild odor. Shrimp may be purchased raw or cooked, peeled or unpeeled, and fresh or frozen. When buying frozen shrimp make sure the shrimp are solidly frozen, have little or no odor, no brown spots and no sign of freezer burn, indicated by a very white, dry appearance around the edges.

HOW MUCH TO BUY

Generally speaking, two pounds of raw, headless, unpeeled shrimp, properly cooked will yield one pound of cooked, peeled, de-veined shrimp, enough for six people. For maximum quality cook fresh shrimp within two days of purchase. If you plan on using it later than two days after purchase, it is better to maintain freshness by freezing on the day of purchase. Cooked shrimp may be stored in the refrigerator for two to three days. Raw, headless shrimp in the shell maintain quality during freezing longer than frozen cooked shrimp. Fresh shrimp can be frozen in a block of ice or glazed. Shrimp frozen commercially maintain quality for six months where home frozen shrimp should be used within a month after freezing.
Thaw frozen shrimp by either placing in refrigerator or under cold running water. NEVER thaw at room temperature or refreeze.

SIMMER
Even though shrimp cooked by this method are commonly referred to as "boiled shrimp", shrimp or any other seafood should not be boiled. Care should be taken not to overcook shrimp, and the liquid in which the shrimp are cooked should only simmer, never boil with the shrimp in it. The sizes of shrimp vary, so it is best to test for doneness near the end of the recommended cooking time for each size to prevent overcooking. Overcooking toughens the protein, dries out the shrimp and causes loss of valuable weight. A shrimp is done when it has lost its translucent, watery appearance in the center and has become opaque and white.

Shrimp may be simmered before or after cleaning depending on personal preference. Usually people will eat more boiled shrimp when the shrimp is served peeled and de-veined. If they have to work at peeling their own they usually don't eat as much. While raw shrimp are easier to clean, cooking a shrimp with the shell on gives the cooked shrimp a richer pink color and a more natural curve. Cooking time varies slightly between peeled and unpeeled shrimp. The cleaned shrimp require a little closer attention to avoid overcooking. The amount of salt is the largest variation, in that the shrimp simmered in the shell require ¼ cup of salt while the peeled and de-veined shrimp only require 2 tablespoons.

BOILED SHRIMP

2 pounds raw, headless, unpeeled shrimp (fresh or frozen)
5 cups water
2 tablespoons salt

Thaw shrimp if frozen. Peel and de-vein shrimp. Rinse thoroughly and drain. Add salt to water and bring to a boil. Add shrimp and reduce heat. Cover and simmer 3 to 4 minutes or until the largest shrimp is opaque in the center when tested by cutting in half. (cooking time will vary according to size of the shrimp; jumbo shrimp will require a little longer cooking time.) Drain shrimp. Rinse shrimp thoroughly for 1 to 2 minutes under cold running water. Serve warm or cold with a Shrimp Sauce or Cocktail Sauce found in chapter 15. Yields one pound cooked shrimp.

Variation: Shrimp may also be boiled in seasoned water by using a commercially packaged blend of spices designated for boiling shrimp such as Zatarain's® or Old Bay®.

**My mother used to add cut lemon slices to the water to reduce the fishy smell when cooking, it also added a mild flavor. **

SHRIMP AND FRUIT SALAD

1 pound cooked, peeled, de-veined shrimp (fresh or frozen)
2 cups diced, unpeeled fresh pears
2 cups diced unpeeled fresh red apples
1 cup thinly sliced celery
½ cup mayonnaise or salad dressing
2 tablespoons milk
1 tablespoon cider vinegar
2 teaspoons grated onion
1 teaspoon salt
Salad greens
Paprika

Thaw shrimp if frozen. Cut large shrimp in half. Combine shrimp, pears, apples, and celery. Combine mayonnaise, milk vinegar, onion and salt. Mix well. Pour over shrimp mixture and toss lightly. Chill for at least 30 minutes. Serve on salad greens. Sprinkle with paprika. Makes 6 servings.

Variation: substitute 2 cups diced fresh pineapple for the pears. Chill salad and dressing separately and add dressing to shrimp mixture just before serving; toss lightly. Serve in fresh pineapple shells or in lettuce cups.

SHRIMP SANDWICH

¾ pound cooked, peeled, de-veined shrimp (fresh or frozen)
2 hard cooked eggs, chopped
½ cup finely chopped celery
1/3 cup mayonnaise or salad dressing
2 tablespoons chopped sweet pickle or drained sweet pickle relish
1 tablespoon grated onion
1 teaspoon salt
½ teaspoon pepper
12 slices sandwich bread
3 tablespoons mayonnaise or salad dressing

Thaw shrimp if frozen. Chop shrimp finely. Combine shrimp, eggs, celery, 1/3 cup mayonnaise, sweet pickle, onion, salt and pepper. Chill. Spread bread slices with remaining 3 tablespoons of mayonnaise. Spread 6 slices of bread with approximately ¼ cup shrimp mixture. Cover with remaining 6 slices of bread. Makes 6 servings.

Variations:
For party sandwiches, trim crust from bread, omit 3 tablespoons of mayonnaise. Instead spread bread lightly with soft butter. Color may be added by using 1 slice of brown bread and 1 slice of white bread for each sandwich. Cut sandwiches into ribbons, triangles or squares. Sandwiches which are prepared in advance should be covered with a damp towel and refrigerated.

Shrimp salad; the above sandwich filing makes a delicious salad. However, dicing or slicing, rather than chopping ingredients would make a more attractive dish. Combine all ingredients, omitting bread and 3 tablespoons of mayonnaise, serve in lettuce cups and sprinkle with paprika.

SHRIMP AND BROCCOLI CASSEROLE

1 pound cooked, peeled, de-veined shrimp (fresh or frozen)
1/3 cup finely chopped onion
½ cup melted butter
2 tablespoons chopped parsley
2 tablespoons lemon juice
¾ teaspoon tarragon leaves
½ teaspoon salt
2 ½ cups chopped broccoli or broccoli spears, cooked and drained
¼ cup fine corn flake crumbs
¼ cup grated Parmesan cheese
Lemon or tomato wedges (garnish)

Thaw shrimp if frozen. Cut large shrimp in half. Cook onion in butter until tender, but not brown. Add shrimp; heat. Stir in parsley, lemon juice tarragon and salt. Place equal amounts of chopped broccoli or quartered broccoli spears into 6 well greased, 10 ounce baking dishes or ramekins. Top each with an equal amount of shrimp mixture. Combine crumbs and cheese; mix well. Sprinkle over shrimp mixture. Bake in a moderate oven at 350 degrees, for 12 to 15 minutes or until thoroughly heated. Garnish with lemon or tomato wedges. Makes 6 servings.

QUICK AND EASY SHRIMP

1 pound cooked, peeled, de-veined shrimp (fresh or frozen)
1 medium green pepper, cut into strips
1 medium onion, sliced
1 clove garlic, minced
2 tablespoons melted butter
1 can (10 and 3/4 ounces) condensed tomato soup
1/3 cup water
2 teaspoons lemon juice
¼ teaspoon salt

Dash pepper
Dash liquid hot pepper sauce
3 cups cooked rice

Thaw shrimp if frozen. Cut large shrimp in half. In a 10-inch fry pan cook green pepper onion and garlic in butter until tender. Add soup, water, lemon juice, salt, pepper, and liquid hot pepper sauce. Simmer 8 to 10 minutes; stirring occasionally. Add shrimp and heat thoroughly. Serve over rice. Makes 6 servings

BROIL

Shrimp may be cooked by the direct heat of broiling, but they are even more likely than fish to dry out and become tough if overcooked, so take care not to overcook and baste frequently during cooking.

SHRIMP KABOBS

1 ½ pounds raw, peeled, de-veined shrimp (fresh or frozen)
4 slices bacon, cut into 1 inch lengths
½ cup (4 ounces) button mushrooms
1 green pepper, cut into 1 inch squares
3 tablespoons melted butter
½ teaspoon salt
Dash pepper

Thaw shrimp if frozen. Partially cook bacon. Place a shrimp, a bacon square, a mushroom and a green pepper square on a short skewer. Place kabobs on a well greased broiler pan. Combine butter, salt and pepper and brush on kabobs. Broil about 3 inches from source of heat for 5 minutes. Turn kabobs and baste. Broil 3 to 5 minutes longer. Makes approximately 24 short skewer kabobs.

GRILLED SHRIMP AND SCALLOPS WITH PICANTE SAUCE

Sauce:
1 Tbsp. olive oil
3 medium tomatoes, chopped (about 1 ½ cups)
1 fresh jalapeno pepper, stemmed, seeded, and chopped (1 Tbsp.)
1 fresh yellow hot pepper, stemmed, seeded and chopped (1 tbsp.)
1 tsp. Lemon juice
3 green onions, chopped
2 cloves garlic, minced or crushed
2 tbsp. dry sherry
¼ tsp. Salt
¼ tsp. Fresh ground black pepper
½ cup chopped fresh cilantro

To make sauce, heat the 1 Tbsp. olive oil in a medium sauce pan. When hot, add chopped tomatoes, jalapeno pepper, yellow hot pepper, lemon juice, green onions, 2 cloves garlic, 2 Tbsp. sherry, salt and pepper. Cook over medium heat until mixture begins to simmer. Simmer 5 minutes, stirring frequently. Turn off heat and stir in cilantro keep warm until ready to serve.

Baste:
2 Tbsp. dry sherry
1 tsp. Olive oil
1 clove garlic, minced or crushed
Combine all the ingredients, stir and set aside.

On the Grill

12 large shrimp, peeled and de-veined
12 large sea scallops
Skewer the scallops and the shrimp on long metal or bamboo skewers, alternating. Or cook in enclosed metal grill baskets. Heat barbecue grill to medium low heat. Cook seafood, brushing frequently with

basting liquid. Do not allow seafood to burn. Shrimp are done when they turn pink and tails curl up. Scallops are done when white and firm to touch when pushed with a finger. Serve shrimp and scallops with about 1 cup sauce. Makes 4 servings.

FRY

Shrimp can be breaded or battered and pan fried or deep fried. Most people prefer to deep fry since a large quantity of shrimp can be cooked quickly and served hot. Both of the following breading or batter recipes are great for shrimp. For a choice of oils see the fish frying section.

FRENCH FRIED SHRIMP

1 ½ pounds raw, peeled, de-veined shrimp (fresh or frozen)
2 eggs, beaten
1 teaspoon salt
½ cup all purpose flour
½ cup dry bread crumbs
½ teaspoon paprika
Oil for deep frying
Shrimp or Tartar sauce

Thaw shrimp if frozen. Combine eggs and salt. Combine flour, dry bread crumbs and paprika. Dip each shrimp in egg, and then roll in crumb mixture. Fry in a basket in deep fat at 350 degrees for 2 to 3 minutes or until golden brown. Drain on absorbent paper. Serve with Shrimp or Tartar Sauce. Makes 6 servings. **Variation:** beat together 1 egg, 2 tablespoons evaporated milk, and 1 teaspoon salt. Dip shrimp in egg mixture and roll in 1 cup fine cracker crumbs (cracker meal) or fine corn flake crumbs. Fry in oil or oven fry.

Variation 2: 1 egg, 1 tablespoon minced onion, ¼ teaspoon garlic salt, ½ cup flour, 1 lb. raw, deveined, and peeled shrimp. Beat egg in bowl, add shrimp to coat, then add garlic salt, onion, and flour. Stir to coat shrimp. Drop shrimp in hot oil, brown on all sides. Drain, then salt to taste.

To oven fry; (for those who don't want to fry in oil) Bread shrimp according to instructions for frying. Instead of deep fat, melt ¼ cup butter in a baking pan 15x10x1 inches. Dip each shrimp in butter and turn quickly to coat both sides. Bake in an extremely hot oven at 500 degrees for 8 to 10 minutes.

BATTER FRIED SHRIMP

1 ½ pounds raw, peeled, de-veined shrimp (fresh or frozen)
½ cup cooking oil
1 egg beaten
1 cup all purpose flour
½ cup milk
¼ cup water
¾ teaspoon seasoned salt
¼ teaspoon salt
Oil for deep frying (I recommend peanut oil)

Thaw shrimp if frozen. Combine cooking oil and egg; beat well. Add remaining ingredients and stir until well blended. Dip each shrimp in the batter. Drop shrimp in hot, oil at 350 degrees and fry for ½ to 1 minute or until golden brown. Remove with slotted spoon; drain on absorbent paper. Serve immediately. Makes 6 servings.

STEAM

Shrimp Pilau is also referred to a Shrimp "Perlo" and is a dish consisting of rice, spices and meat or seafood, in this case shrimp. Since most of the liquid is absorbed when the shrimp are added, the shrimp are cooked by conduction of heat and the steam produced from the hot rice. This is a little different from the common method of steaming food.

SHRIMP PILAU

1 pound raw, peeled, de-veined shrimp (fresh or frozen)
3 slices bacon, cut into small pieces
1 cup chopped green pepper
¼ cup chopped onion
2 cups (16 ounces) whole tomatoes
¾ cup water
¾ cup uncooked rice
1 teaspoon salt
1/8 teaspoon pepper
1/8 teaspoon thyme

Thaw shrimp if frozen. Cut large shrimp in half. In a 2-quart sauce pan, cook bacon until crisp. Remove bacon. Cook green pepper and onion in bacon fat until tender. Break tomatoes into small pieces removing tough centers. Add tomatoes and water and bring to a boil. Stir in rice and seasonings. Reduce heat. Cover and cook rice mixture over low heat for 18 to 20 minutes. Mix in shrimp, cover and continue cooking for 10 to 12 minutes or until shrimp are tender. Garnish with bacon. Makes 6 servings. Variation; substitute one 5-ounce package of yellow rice with seasonings for ¾ cup of uncooked rice.

HAMP AND RAE'S SHRIMP CREOLE

1 ½ lbs. shrimp (fresh or frozen)
¼ cup chopped onion
¼ cup chopped green pepper
¼ cup chopped celery, fine chopped
1 clove garlic, finely chopped
¼ cup butter
1 tsp. crushed red pepper
1 tsp. Chili powder
Dash of black pepper
1 tsp. Salt

1 bay leaf (remove after 10 minutes)
2 or 3 Tbsp. flour
2 cups canned tomato wedges,
or fresh chopped tomatoes

Peel shrimp, remove sand veins and wash. Cut large shrimp in half. Cook onion, green pepper, and garlic in butter until tender: blend in flour and seasonings. Add tomatoes and cook until thick, stirring constantly. Then let simmer about 20 minutes with shrimp in uncovered pan. Serve over rice. This sauce can also be used without the shrimp. Just serve over rice with baked or broiled fish.

CHAPTER TEN --FLORIDA LOBSTER

A Florida original, the Florida Crawfish or lobster is different from the northern lobsters in that the meat comes from the tail instead of the claws. It is a delicacy that divers turn out for annually in south Florida from West Palm Beach to Key West to harvest. Best when cooked and eaten fresh, they can also be cooked and frozen. When preparing cooked frozen lobster note the membrane surrounding the meat for toughness and remove if necessary. When buying lobster figure a one-pound whole lobster per person, but when mixing with other ingredients it may be stretched to serve six. Generally, a one-pound lobster when cooked will yield 1/3 pound of meat. If not planning to cook fresh lobster when purchased, freeze whole. Since the shell protects the meat from drying out there is no need for glazing or block freezing.

SIMMER
Be sure to cook lobster, like other seafood, just below the boiling point. Boiling will toughen and dry out moisture and destroy delicate texture.

Boiled Florida Lobster

2 live lobsters (1 pound each) or
2 frozen whole green lobster (1 pound each)
3 quarts boiling water
3 tablespoons salt
Clarified butter

Thaw lobster if frozen. In a 6-quart saucepan, bring water and salt to a boil. Plunge live lobster headfirst (or place thawed green lobster) into boiling salted water. Cover and return to simmer for 12 to 15 minutes. Larger lobster will require a little longer cooking time. Drain. Rinse with cold water for 1 to 2 minutes. Split and clean lobster. Serve with clarified butter. Makes 2 servings.

Variation: Brush split boiled lobster tails with 1 tbs. butter. Sprinkle with 1/8 tsp pepper and 1/8 tsp paprika. **Broil** 4 inches from heat for 5 minutes or until browned. Make dip of ¼ cup butter and 1 tablespoon lemon juice to serve with lobsters

Frozen spiny lobster tails can be cooked by the above method. Increase salt to ½ cup for six spiny lobster tails (5 to 8 ounces each). Reduce cooking time to 5 to 10 minutes depending on size. Drain. Rinse in cold water for 1 minute. Cut in half lengthwise and serve with clarified butter.

Variation: Crawfish may also be boiled in seasoned water by using a commercially packaged blend of spices designated for boiling crawfish such as Zatarain's® or Old Bay®.

STEAM

To serve cold cooked lobster meat with clarified butter, steam just long enough to heat. If the cooked lobster is frozen, thaw, clean and rinse body cavity thoroughly. Place whole lobster or lobster tails on a rack in a covered saucepan or steamer containing a small amount of boiling water. Do not immerse rack in water. Steam just long enough to heat lobster meat thoroughly. Serve immediately in the shell.

Although boiling cooked lobster is a common practice, steaming is the preferred method for heating cold, cooked lobster, as steaming retains the natural moisture and delicate texture of the meat. For the Newberg and Kokomo recipes requiring cooked lobster meat, remove meat from the shell and follow recipe instructions.

LOBSTER NEWBURG

1 pound cooked lobster meat (fresh or frozen)
¼ cup butter
2 tablespoons all purpose flour
¾ teaspoon salt
¼ teaspoon paprika
Dash cayenne pepper
1 pint Half & Half cream
2 egg yolks, beaten
1 ½ to 2 tablespoons sherry
Toast points

Thaw lobster if frozen. Cut lobster meat into ½ inch pieces. Melt butter; blend in flour, salt, paprika, and pepper. Add Half & Half cream gradually and cook, stirring constantly, until thick and smooth. Stir a little of the hot sauce into the egg yolks; add egg yolks to remaining sauce, stirring constantly. Add lobster meat; heat. Remove from heat and slowly stir in sherry. Serve immediately on toast points. Makes 6 servings.

KOKOMO LOBSTER

1 pound cooked lobster meat (fresh or frozen)
6 ounces mushrooms
1 small onion, finely chopped
¼ cup melted butter
1 cup sour cream
2 tablespoons chopped parsley
¼ teaspoon salt
Dash cayenne pepper
Patty shells or toast points

Thaw lobster if frozen. Cut lobster meat into bite sizes pieces. Cook mushrooms and onion in butter until tender but not brown. Add lobster, sour cream parsley, salt and pepper. Heat thoroughly, not allowing mixture to boil. Serve in patty shells or on toast points. Makes 6 servings.

Two addition ways to serve lobster over rice, on toast points or in patty shells are **Lobster Au Gratin** and **Lobster Hollandaise**.

For **Lobster Au Gratin,** prepare a rich cheese sauce, add a dash of cayenne pepper and one pound cooked lobster meat cut into bite sized pieces, and heat thoroughly.

Lobster Hollandaise is also easy to prepare. Follow the directions on package and prepare two packages of hollandaise sauce mix. Add 1/3 cup milk gradually, stirring constantly, and a dash of cayenne pepper. Add one-pound lobster meat cut into bite sized pieces and heat thoroughly. Serve immediately over rice, toast points or in patty shells. Sprinkle with paprika. Makes 6 servings.

LOBSTER THERMIDOR

1 pound cooked lobster meat (fresh or frozen)
2 tablespoons butter
2 tablespoons all purpose flour
1½ teaspoons dry mustard
½ teaspoon salt
Dash cayenne pepper
1 ½ cups Half and Half
½ cup (4 ounces) mushrooms
2 tablespoons grated Parmesan cheese
Paprika

Thaw lobster if frozen. Cut lobster meat into ½ inch pieces. Melt butter in 10-inch fry pan. Blend in flour and seasonings. Add cream gradually and cook stirring constantly, until thick and smooth. Add mushrooms and lobster meat.

Serve in reserved cleaned and rinsed lobster shells from which the meat is removed or into 6 well-greased, 6-ounce baking shells.

Sprinkle with cheese and paprika. Bake in a hot oven at 400 degrees for 10 minutes, or until top is lightly browned. Makes 6 servings.

LOBSTER ENCHILADA

1 lobster, 1 green pepper, 1 pimiento, olive oil, boiled rice.

Boil lobster 20 minutes then remove meat. Cut green pepper and pimiento into strips and fry until tender in small amount of olive oil. Add lobster meat. Serve with boiled rice.

FLORIDA LOBSTER SALAD

¾ pound cooked lobster meat (fresh or frozen)
6 cups lettuce, torn into small pieces
2 medium tomatoes, cut into bite sized pieces
1 cup grated Cheddar cheese
½ cup sliced pitted ripe olives
1/3 cup sliced green onions and tops
½ cup creamy Caesar salad dressing
Whole pitted ripe olives (garnish)

Thaw lobster if frozen. Remove lobster from shells. Cut lobster into ½ inch pieces. Combine lobster, lettuce, tomatoes, cheese, olives and green onion. Add dressing and toss lightly. Garnish with whole ripe olives. Serve immediately. Makes 6 servings.

BAKE

Raw lobster is tender and moist when meat is frequently basted or completely covered with stuffing during baking. This simple stuffing enhances the flavor of the lobster meat. Another delicious stuffing is the basic blue crab stuffing in the crab section.

BAKED STUFFED LOBSTER

2 live lobster (1 pound each) or 2 frozen green lobster (1 pound each)
1 ½ cups soft bread crumbs
½ cup grated Cheddar cheese
2 tablespoons melted butter
1 tablespoon grated onion
Paprika

Thaw lobster if frozen. Cut lobster in half lengthwise. Remove the stomach and intestinal vein. Rinse and clean body cavity thoroughly. Combine bread crumbs, cheese, butter and onion. Place stuffing in body cavity and spread over surface of the tail meat. Place on a baking pan, 15x10x1 inches. Bake in a hot oven at 400 degrees for 15 to 20 minutes, or until lightly browned. Makes 2 servings.

CHAPTER ELEVEN---BLUE CRABS

The blue crab has five pairs of legs with the first pair always equipped with pincers. A fully grown blue crab averages 5 to 7 inches across the shell. To identify the sex of a blue crab turn it over and look at the abdomen, if it is shaped like a "T" it is a male. The female's abdomen is shaped like a "V", there may also be visible mass of orange eggs attached. If you find a female with eggs attached, DO NOT harvest as it is illegal!

All along Florida's coast you can find these delicacies, either to buy commercially or to be taken by a crab net for an afternoon of fun with a delicious reward. Packaged, pasteurized crab meat can also be purchased in the following forms;

Lump meat: that is solid lumps of white meat from the back fin of the body;

Special or flake meat: small pieces of white meat from the body; **Claw meat:** a brownish tinted meat from the claws used in recipes where appearance is not important. Crab fingers can also be breaded (using the breading from Breaded Scallops recipe) and deep fried for 30 to 45 seconds or until golden brown; or batter-fried (use the batter-fried shrimp batter) and deep fried for 8 to 10 seconds or until golden brown. Plain or fried, crab fingers and a seafood sauce make a delicious main dish or hors d'oeuvre.

If crabs are purchased live make sure they show movement. Allow three crabs per person. One pound of lump, special or claw is enough to feed six people.

SIMMER

Simmering or steaming is a method used to cook all blue crab meat with the exception of the soft shelled crab which can be grilled or fried. All of the following recipes are ways to use cooked blue crab meat.

BOILED BLUE CRAB

24 live hard shell crabs
6 quarts boiling water
1/3 cup salt

Place live crabs in boiling salted water. Cover and return to the boiling point. Reduce heat, and simmer for 12 to 15 minutes. Drain. Rinse in cold water. Serve hot or cold. Makes 6 servings.
Variation: Crabs may also be boiled in seasoned water by using a commercially packaged blend of spices designated for boiling crab such as Zatarain's® or Old Bay®.

Crabs may also be cleaned prior to cooking and only the claws and inner skeleton (or pod) which contains the white body meat cooked. However, the cooking time should be reduced to 5 to 7 minutes.

BASIC BLUE CRAB STUFFING

1 pound blue crab meat, fresh or canned
½ cup chopped onion
1/3 cup chopped celery
1/3 cup chopped green pepper
2 cloves garlic, minced
1/3 cup melted butter
2 cups soft bread crumbs
3 eggs, beaten
1 tablespoon chopped parsley

1 teaspoon salt
½ teaspoon pepper

Remove any pieces of shell or cartilage from crabmeat. Cook onion, celery green pepper and garlic in butter until tender but not brown. Combine all ingredients and mix well.

*** Makes enough stuffing for six flounder, ¾ pound each or one 4-pound flounder.
Variations: This basic stuffing can be augmented to make the crab cakes or deviled crab.

CRAB CAKES: To the basic stuffing mixture add 1 teaspoon prepared horseradish (if you want very hot crab cakes replace the horseradish with 1 ½ teaspoons of commercially blended, powdered seafood seasoning), 1 teaspoon Worcestershire sauce, and ¼ teaspoon dry mustard. If the mixture seems too dry, add a little mayonnaise. Divide mixture equally to form 6 large or 12 small cakes. Roll cakes in 1 cup soft bread crumbs. Place cakes in a heavy fry pan containing 1/8 inch fat, hot but not smoking. Fry at moderate heat until brown on both sides. Makes 6 servings.

DEVILED CRAB: To the basic stuffing add 1 can (10 ¾ ounces) condensed cream of mushroom soup, ½ teaspoon Worcestershire sauce ½ teaspoon dry mustard and ¼ teaspoon liquid hot pepper sauce. Mix well and place mixture in six individual shallow baking dishes or 12 crab shells. Bake in a moderate oven at 375 degrees for 15 to 20 minutes or until heated thoroughly. Makes 6 servings.

STUFFED LOBSTER, SHRIMP, OR FLOUNDER; this basic stuffing recipe is good with all three but particularly interesting when stuffed and baked in a flounder. To prepare the flounder, place light side down and make a cut with a sharp knife lengthwise down the center of the dark side about one inch from the gills to one inch from the tail. Then tilt the knife sideways to cut horizontally along the backbone on each side to form a pocket in which the crab mixture can be stuffed.

Many people enjoy crabmeat cold, fresh from the can, or steamed just long enough to heat it and serve with melted butter. You can do many creative things with crabmeat to spice up a seafood meal, from adding crabmeat to cheese sauce to put on fish or over toast points.

CRAB BISQUE

1 pound blue crab meat, fresh or canned
2 tablespoons finely chopped onion
2 tablespoons finely chopped celery
¼ cup melted butter
3 tablespoons all purpose flour
1 teaspoon salt
¼ teaspoon paprika
Dash white pepper
1 quart milk
¼ cup chopped parsley

Remove any pieces of shell or cartilage from crabmeat. Cook onion and celery in butter until tender but not brown. Blend in flour and seasonings. Add milk gradually, stirring constantly; cook until thick. Add crabmeat and heat. Just before serving, sprinkle with parsley. Makes 6 servings.

VEGGIE BLUE CRAB SANDWICH

1-pound blue crab meat, fresh or canned
1 cup sliced almonds
½ cup chopped celery
½ cup mayonnaise or salad dressing
2 tablespoons lemon juice
12 toasted, buttered English muffin halves
24 cooked asparagus spears (more if desired)
6 slices (1 ounce each) Cheddar cheese
Paprika
Tomato wedges

Remove any shell or cartilage from crabmeat. Combine crabmeat, almonds, celery, mayonnaise, and lemon juice. Arrange muffin halves on a cookie sheet, 15x12 inches. Place two or more asparagus spears on each muffin half. Cover asparagus and muffin with approximately 1/3 cup of crab mixture. Cut each cheese slice diagonally into quarters. Place 2 triangles on each sandwich. Sprinkle with paprika.

Bake in a 400 degree oven for 15 to 20 minutes or a microwave until heated thoroughly and cheese is melted. Serve with tomato wedges. Makes 6 servings.

CHAPTER TWELVE--STONE CRAB

The Florida stone crab is the only stone crab harvested commercially in the United States. Florida law prohibits the taking of the crab body so fishermen will harvest one or both claws from the crab and return the crab to the water to regenerate a new claw for future harvest. Claws are removed at the joints to protect the crab from bleeding. When the claws are removed properly the crab can regenerate the lost claw up to four times during its lifecycle. Because raw claw meat sticks to the shell when frozen, stone crab claws are cooked immediately upon landing. Cooked claws can then be frozen in the shell. You can then purchase stone crab claws frozen or refrigerated. Freshness is usually determined by a mild odor. The meat of the stone crab is very rich and delicious, so when buying its best to figure three large claws per person. Store in refrigerator and use within two to three days. If you buy them fresh cooked and frozen in the same day, they will last in the freezer for six months. When freezing examine the shell for any cracks and only freeze those with intact shells. Thaw frozen claws in the refrigerator for 12 to 18 hours before serving, running under cold water or at room temperature will reduce quality.

Serving stone crab claws is a treat in itself that everyone can get involved; I usually place the claw in a kitchen towel before cracking to catch any bits of shell or juices from inside the shell then crack all the sections of shell with a hammer or nutcracker. Let hungry guests pick out the meat for themselves. The claw portion also makes an attractive hors d'oeuvre or appetizer, to serve crack the claw and remove the shell and movable pincer leaving the meat attached to the remaining pincer. The cooked meat can also be picked from the shell and used in any recipe calling for cooked crabmeat or lobster. Approximately 2 ½ pounds of cooked stone crab claws are required to yield one pound of crabmeat.

Stone crab is best eaten cold or steamed only long enough to heat and served with clarified butter or warm lemon butter. Another treat is to eat them with a warm mustard sauce (see chapter 15 for sauces).

MANGO MARINATED STONE CRAB CLAWS

3 pounds medium stone crab claws
2 cups ripe mango, cut into 1/2 inch cubes
3 tablespoons cilantro, finely chopped
2 jalapeño peppers, seeded and minced
4 tablespoons lime juice
1 tablespoon light brown sugar
salad greens

Crack claws and remove shell and movable pincer, leaving the meat attached to the remaining pincer. Place in a single layer in a shallow dish.

To make salsa marinade: combine mango, cilantro, peppers, lime juice and sugar in a mixing bowl. Taste for seasoning, adding more lime juice and/or brown sugar as needed.

Spoon the salsa mixture over the meaty part of crab claws.
Cover and marinate in refrigerator at least 2 hours.
Serve claws on a bed of salad greens with mango salsa as an appetizer.

There are many different sauces that can be used for dipping when eating stone crab claws. Besides clarified or lemon butter, you can use a mustard sauce, a hot or cool sauce, or a sweet and sour sauce. (See Ch. 15)

CHAPTER THIRTEEN---OYSTERS

Florida oysters, particularly Apalachicola and Cedar Key oysters are world renown. They are sold live in the shell, fresh, frozen and canned. Oysters must be live when purchased in the shell which is indicated by shells that close tightly when handled. Live oysters are sold by the dozens or by the bag which contains one bushel. When purchasing live oysters, in the shell, figure three dozen to feed six people. Live oysters will remain live for seven to ten days if stored at 35 to 40 degrees. Shucked oysters are graded and sold by size, usually in pints or gallons. The largest shucked oysters are sold as "selects", while the average sized oysters are sold as "standards". One pint of shucked oysters will yield six servings. When serving fried or on the half shell, people may eat more! A fresh oyster is plump and has a natural creamy color and clear liquid. Fresh shucked oysters will last in the refrigerator for a week. When frozen at home, oysters lose some of their quality and should be used for casseroles, stuffing, or fried upon thawing. Home freezing oysters is not recommended, but commercial quick frozen oysters are fine. If you do decide to freeze your own, do so in the container they were purchased in their own liquor or a container that allows little airspace. Use frozen oysters within two months if possible. Cooked oysters should never be home frozen. Thaw frozen oysters in the refrigerator or in an airtight container under cold running water. Once thawed, they should not be refrozen.

Oysters are easy to prepare and entirely edible, they are delicious raw or cooked in a variety of recipes. To retain the delicate, distinctive flavor of oysters, only cook long enough to heat thoroughly and maintain their natural plumpness and tender quality.

Warning: People with compromised immune systems are at high-risk and should avoid consumption of raw oysters. They can, however, consume thoroughly cooked oysters. If you have chronic illness of the liver, stomach, blood, diabetes or other immune disorders, you are at greater risk of serious illness from raw oysters and should eat oysters fully cooked. People in high-risk groups insistent on consuming raw oysters should consider only oysters that are labeled "processed to reduce Vibrio vulnificus to non-detectable levels." If unsure of your risk, consult a physician.

BROIL

Broil only as long as required to cook other ingredients and heat oysters thoroughly. Since oysters consist primarily of water (or liquor), overcooking must be avoided or valuable weight, moisture and nutrition will be lost during shrinkage.

BROILED OYSTERS

36 oysters, raw in the shell
¼ cup soft bread crumbs
½ teaspoon salt
1/8 teaspoon pepper
1/8 teaspoon paprika
4 slices bacon, cut in small pieces

Shuck and drain oysters. Place oysters on deep half shell, removing any remaining shell particles. Combine bread crumbs, salt, pepper and paprika and sprinkle over oysters. Place an equal amount of bacon pieces on top of each oyster. Place oysters on a broiler pan, 15x10x1 inches. Broil about 3 inches from source of heat for 5 to 7 minutes or until edges curl and bacon is brown. Makes 6 servings.

FRY

Pan-frying requires more time for cooking and browning than deep frying. If oysters are deep fried, cooking time at 360 degrees will be one to three minutes or just long enough to brown the coating. To deep fry one pint of oysters, dip oysters in a mixture of 2 well beaten eggs, 2 tablespoons milk, 1 teaspoon salt, and 1/8 teaspoon pepper. Roll oysters in 1 cup bread crumbs, cracker crumbs or cornmeal. Having all the oysters breaded in advance of cooking makes frying quicker, easier and allows all the oysters to be served hot. The Apalachicola Oyster Fry is a little extra trouble, but well worth the effort.

APALACHICOLA OYSTER FRY

1 pint oysters (fresh or frozen)
2 eggs
2 tablespoons evaporated milk
¼ teaspoon salt
1/3 cup flour
2 cups saltine cracker crumbs
1/3 cup butter
1/3 cup cooking oil

Thaw oysters if frozen; drain. Beat together eggs, milk and salt. Dip oysters into egg mixture then lightly into flour. Dip into egg mixture again and roll in cracker crumbs. Let stand 5 to 10 minutes before frying. Heat the butter and oil in a large fry pan over moderate heat at 350 degrees. Fry oysters 5 to 7 minutes or until lightly browned, turning once during cooking. Remove from oil and drain on absorbent paper towels. Serve with favorite seafood sauce. Makes 6 servings.

SIMMER

Cooking oysters in their own liquor and using the liquor in the recipe as part of the required liquid adds more oyster flavor and retains the water soluble nutrients.

CREAMED OYSTERS

1 pint oysters (fresh or frozen)
2 packages (1 ounce each) white wine sauce mix
½ teaspoon Worcestershire sauce
¼ teaspoon liquid hot pepper sauce
Paprika
Parsley

Thaw oysters if frozen. Simmer oysters in their own liquor about 5 minutes or until edges curl. Remove oysters and reserve liquor. Prepare sauce mix according to package directions using reserved oyster liquor in place of water. If there is not enough liquid, add water to complete volume called for in package directions. Add oysters and heat. Serve in patty shells or on toast points. Sprinkle with paprika and garnish with parsley. Makes 6 servings.

Variation: Use the basic creamed oysters, 3 cups cooked macaroni and 1 cup grated Cheddar cheese to make oyster au gratin:

OYSTER AU GRATIN

Place 1 ½ cups cooked macaroni in a well greased 1 ½ quart casserole. Top with a layer of creamed oysters and ½ cup grated Cheddar cheese. Repeat layers. Bake at 350 degrees 12 to 15 minutes or until heated thoroughly. Makes 6 servings

To the basic Creamed Oysters, add 2 chopped hard boiled eggs, 3 ounces sliced mushrooms and 1 cup green peas. Serving suggestions:

(1) Serve over toast points or in patty shells; (2) Spoon into a pie shell and cover with a top crust. Bake at 400 degrees for 12 to 15 minutes or until crust is golden brown; (3) Pour into a well-greased, 1-quart casserole and top with cooked biscuits. 6 servings.

OYSTER STEW

1 pint oysters (fresh or frozen)
1 quart milk
1 ½ teaspoons salt
1/8 teaspoon pepper & paprika

Thaw oysters if frozen. Drain oysters, reserving liquor. Remove any remaining shell particles. Add oysters and liquor to margarine and cook 3 minutes or until edges of oysters begin to curl. Add milk, salt, and pepper; heat thoroughly but do not boil. Garnish with paprika. Serve at once. Makes 6 servings.

Variation 1: Use 1 ½ pints oysters, 4 tablespoon butter, 1 cup milk and 2 cups heavy cream or half and half. Season to taste.
Variation 2: To make chunky chowder, along with one quart of milk, add ½ cup sautéed chopped onion, ½ cup sautéed sliced celery, 1 cup (8 ounces) whole kernel corn, and 1 cup cooked diced potatoes. Makes 6 servings.

ROAST

Roasting is cooking uncovered in hot air and when used as a method for cooking seafood, is usually done outside around a fire or over hot coals.

To roast oysters, wash them thoroughly. Place oysters on a grill about 4 inches from hot coals. Roast 10 to 15 minutes or until shell begins to open. Serve in shells with melted butter or any favorite seafood sauce.

BAKE

Oysters are delicious when baked because the liquor is retained in the recipe. To retain natural plumpness and tenderness cook only long enough to heat thoroughly.

SCALLOPED OYSTERS

1 pint oysters
2 cups coarse cracker crumbs
½ cup melted butter
½ teaspoon salt
1/8 teaspoon pepper
¼ teaspoon Worcestershire sauce
1 cup milk

Thaw oysters if frozen. Drain oysters. Combine cracker crumbs, butter, salt, and pepper. Reserve 1/3 of mixture for topping. Place another 1/3 of crumb mixture in a well-greased 1-quart casserole; cover with a layer of oysters. Repeat layers. Add Worcestershire sauce to milk, and pour over contents of casserole. Top with reserved 1/3 crumb mixture. Bake in a moderate oven at 350 degrees for 30 minutes or until thoroughly heated. Makes 6 servings.

CHAPTER FOURTEEN--SCALLOPS

The majority of scallops harvested recreationally in Florida are found in Port St Joe/ Cape San Blas areas, Carrabelle, St Marks, Perry, and Steinhatchee. Scallops can propel themselves through the water by snapping their shells together to expel a jet of water. The adductor muscle then becomes oversized leading to the lean, light, firm meat with a sweet flavor that is eaten. There are two types of scallops harvested commercially in Florida, the calico and the bay scallop. Scallops are unable to close their shells tightly and subsequently die soon after harvest. For this reason, they are shucked immediately after harvest and their meat iced. Since only the adductor muscle is eaten, the name scallop has generally come to mean the adductor muscle when used to describe shucked meat.

In choosing fresh scallops examine the product for a creamy white, light, tan, or pinkish color and a mild, slightly sweet odor. When purchased in packages, fresh or frozen scallops should be practically free of liquid. Store the fresh scallops on ice in the refrigerator at 35 to 40 degrees. They are best used on day of purchase, but can be kept on ice for two days with little flavor or texture change. Raw frozen scallops can be kept for three to four months if kept at temperatures of 0 degrees or below. Quality is better if frozen raw. Cooked scallops lose texture, moisture and flavor during freezing. Thaw frozen scallops in refrigerator or under cold running water. After thawing raw scallops should have the mild, slightly sweet odor characteristic of the fresh product.

POACH

Poach scallops just long enough to heat thoroughly. Test for doneness by cutting a large scallop in half and when center is opaque and white, scallops are done. Overcooking causes toughness and valuable weight loss.

BASIC POACHED SCALLOPS

1 ½ pounds calico or bay scallops (fresh or frozen)
2 cups water
3 tablespoons lemon juice
½ teaspoon salt
3 slices onion
Clarified butter

Thaw scallops if frozen. Rinse scallops with cold water to remove any remaining shell particles. Drain. Combine water, lemon juice salt and onion in a 10-inch fry pan and bring to a boil. Add scallops; reduce heat and cover. Cook 2 to 3 minutes, depending on size. Drain scallops. Serve with clarified butter or use in recipes requiring cooked scallops. Yields approximately 1 pound cooked scallops, the minimum required to serve six. Use poached scallops in the Island Scallop Salad on the following page.

ISLAND SCALLOP SALAD

1 pound cooked calico or bay scallops
5 cups shredded lettuce
1 pound asparagus, cooked
1 pint cherry tomatoes cut in half
3 hard boiled eggs, sliced
1 cucumber, sliced
Kent's Scallop Dressing*

Place shredded lettuce in bottom of a large salad bowl. Line ¼ of the edge of bowl with asparagus, ¼ edge with tomatoes, and finish lining edges of bowl with alternating slices of egg and cucumber. Fill the center of the bowl with scallops. Serve with Kent's Scallop Dressing found in chapter 15. Makes 6 servings.

BROIL

Scallops can be broiled but need to be basted well to prevent drying during cooking.

BASIC BROILED SCALLOPS

2 pounds calico or bay scallops (fresh or frozen)
½ cup butter
¾ to 1 teaspoon minced garlic
½ teaspoon salt
1/8 teaspoon white pepper
Paprika

Thaw scallops if frozen. Rinse scallops with cold water to remove any remaining shell particles. Melt butter in small sauce pan. Add garlic and cook over very low heat for 5 minutes; do not brown garlic. Place scallops in a single layer baking dish, m11x7 ½ x1 inches. Sprinkle scallops with salt and pepper. Pour garlic butter over scallops; stir to coat scallops on all sides. Broil about 4 inches from source of heat for 2 minutes. Stir scallops; broil 2 minutes longer. Sprinkle with paprika. Serve immediately. Makes 6 servings.

BAKE

The even heat of baking retains the natural moisture of scallops.

GRASS ISLAND BAKED SCALLOPS

2 pounds' calico or bay scallops (fresh or frozen)
2 cups rich round buttery flavored cracker crumbs (Ritz etc)
¼ cup melted butter
¼ cup ketchup
½ teaspoon salt
¼ teaspoon sugar
Dash pepper
¼ cup sliced green onions and tops (continued on next page)

1 tablespoon melted butter
Paprika

Thaw scallops if frozen. Rinse scallops with cold water to remove any remaining shell particles. Cut large scallops in half. Combine scallops, cracker crumbs, butter, ketchup, salt, sugar, and pepper. Place equal amounts of scallop mixture in 6 well greased, 10 ounce casseroles or place scallop mixture in a shallow 1 ½ quart casserole. Combine green onion and butter; place on top of scallop mixture. Bake in a moderate oven at 350 degrees for 25 to 30 minutes or until brown. Sprinkle with paprika. Makes 6 servings.

FRY

BASIC FRIED SCALLOPS

2 pounds' calico or bay scallops (fresh or frozen)
2 eggs, beaten
2 tablespoons milk
1 teaspoon salt
Dash pepper
½ cup all purpose flour
1 ¼ cup dry bread crumbs
Oil for frying

Thaw scallops if frozen. Rinse scallops with cold water to remove any remaining shell particles. Beat together eggs, milk, salt, and pepper. Roll scallops in flour, dip in egg mixture and roll in dry bread crumbs.

TO PAN FRY: Place breaded scallops in a heavy fry pan which contains approximately ½ inch of oil, hot but not smoking. Fry at moderate heat 350 degrees for approximately 2 to 3 minutes, or until golden brown, turning once during cooking. Drain on absorbent paper. Serve plain or
with a sauce. Makes 6 servings.

TO DEEP FRY: Fry breaded scallops in a basket in oil at a moderate heat 350 degrees for 1 to 2 minutes or until golden brown. Remove from oil and drain on absorbent paper towels. Serve plain or with a sauce.

CAPE SAN BLAS SCALLOP AMANDINE

2 pounds calico or bay scallops (fresh or frozen)
¼ teaspoon salt
Dash pepper
½ cup all purpose flour
½ cup slivered almonds
½ cup melted butter
2 tablespoons chopped parsley

Thaw scallops if frozen. Rinse scallops with cold water to remove any remaining shell particles. Sprinkle scallops with salt and pepper. Roll in flour. Fry almonds in butter until lightly browned. Remove almonds. Add scallops and continue frying. When scallops are brown on one side, turn carefully and brown on the other side. Cooking time is approximately 4 minutes. Add parsley and almonds. Serve immediately. Makes 6 servings.

SMOKED

PEPPERFISH KEYS SMOKED SCALLOP KABOBS

½ pound bay or calico scallops (fresh or frozen)
12 lime slices
4 slices Canadian bacon, cut in half
¼ cup lime juice
¼ cup butter, melted
¼ cup Parmesan cheese
½ teaspoon salt
¼ cup chopped parsley
Parsley (garnish)

Thaw scallops if frozen. Rinse with cold water to remove any shell particles. Using four 10 inch skewers, alternate scallops, lime slices, and Canadian bacon. Combine lime juice and butter; baste scallops. Combine Parmesan cheese, salt and parsley; sprinkle on scallops. Place skewers on well greased grill in smoke oven, about 4 inches from warm coals and wet hickory chips. Cook 4 to 6 minutes or until scallops are tender. Garnish with parsley. Makes 4 servings.

CHAPTER FIFTEEN—SPREADS, DIPS, SAUCES, AND SIDES

KENT'S SMOKED MULLET SPREAD

1 large smoked mullet
3 heaping tablespoons of the following;
Fresh parsley (chopped)
Cream cheese
Crushed pineapple with juice
1 stalk of finely chopped celery (optional)

Mix the cream cheese, parsley and pineapple together in your serving bowl.
Flake the smoked mullet meat then add it to the mixture. Stir well to blend ingredients. Place in refrigerator for 1 hour to chill. Serve with a hearty cracker such as a Ritz®, whole wheat or other fancy cracker.

SMOKED FISH SPREAD

1 ½ pounds of smoked fish
1 ¼ cup mayonnaise or salad dressing
2 tablespoons finely chopped sweet pickle or relish
2 tablespoons chopped parsley
1 tablespoon mustard
2 teaspoons minced onion
2 teaspoons finely chopped celery
1 clove garlic, minced
1/8 teaspoon Worcestershire sauce

Remove skin and bones from fish. Flake the fish well. Combine all ingredients and mix well. Chill at least one hour. Makes approximately 3 ½ cups spread.

SMOKED FISH BUTTER

1 ½ cups, flaked, smoked mullet or other smoked fish
2/3 cup butter, softened
½ teaspoon curry powder
¼ teaspoon salt
¼ teaspoon white pepper
Assorted crackers or raw vegetables

Combine fish, butter, curry powder salt and white pepper in a mixing bowl and beat with an electric mixer until well blended and smooth. Chill at least one hour. Serve with crackers or raw vegetables. Makes approximately 1 ½ cups.

ONION SMOKED FISH SPREAD

2 cups smoked, flaked fish
¾ cups mayonnaise or salad dressing
½ teaspoon onion powder
2 tablespoons chopped parsley
Assorted chips, crackers, or raw vegetables
Chopped parsley (garnish)
In a 1-quart bowl, combine all ingredients except crackers and garnish; chill. Garnish with chopped parsley. Serve with chips, crackers, or raw vegetables. Makes approximately 2 cups dip.

SUMMER HOT SAUCE

½ cup honey
½ cup prepared mustard
½ cup cider vinegar
¼ cup Worcestershire sauce
1 tablespoon chopped parsley
2 teaspoons liquid hot pepper sauce
1 teaspoon salt

In a 1-quart sauce pan, blend honey and mustard; stir in remaining ingredients. Bring to a boil. Serve with smoked fish or shrimp. Makes approximately 1 ½ cups sauce.

JOE COOL SAUCE

¼ cup mayonnaise or salad dressing
1 egg
3 tablespoons lemon juice
1 teaspoon salt
1 teaspoon sugar
1 teaspoon instant minced onion
1 teaspoon mustard
2 drops liquid hot sauce
1/8 teaspoon pepper
¾ cup salad oil
1/3 cup chopped parsley
1 tablespoon horseradish
1 clove garlic, minced

Place first nine ingredients in a blender. Cover, blend for a few seconds; add oil gradually and continue to blend until thick and smooth. Add parsley, horseradish, and garlic. Blend until smooth. Serve with smoked fish. Makes approximately 2 ¼ cups sauce.

SPICY BASTING SAUCE

1/3 cup steak sauce
¼ cup ketchup
¼ cup melted butter
1 tablespoon vinegar
1 teaspoon salt
½ teaspoon curry powder

Combine all ingredients and mix well. Makes enough to baste 2 pounds of fish fillets.

SHRIMP SAUCE

½ cup chili sauce
½ cup ketchup
1 tablespoon lemon juice
2 teaspoons horseradish
Combine all ingredients. Chill. Makes approximately 1 cup sauce.

FLUFFY LEMON SAUCE

2 tablespoons butter
2 tablespoons all purpose flour
½ teaspoon salt
¼ teaspoon paprika
1¼ cup milk
½ cup mayonnaise or salad dressing
2 teaspoons lemon juice
Melt butter in a one-quart saucepan. Blend in flour, salt, and paprika. Add milk gradually and cook, stirring constantly, until thickened. Stir in mayonnaise and lemon juice. Heat, but do not boil. Serve warm over poached or baked fish. Makes approximately 1 ¾ cups sauce. Fluffy Lemon Sauce is easy to prepare and is superb on poached fish.

GINGER BASTING SAUCE

½ cup ketchup
¼ cup chicken broth
2 tablespoons soy sauce
1 tablespoon honey
2 tablespoons fresh grated ginger (Variation: use lemons or limes instead of ginger)
Combine all ingredients. Make's approximately 1 cup sauce.

TARTAR SAUCE

¼ cup mayonnaise or salad dressing
2 tablespoons drained sweet pickle relish
1 teaspoon minced onion
1 teaspoon lemon juice

Combine all ingredients. Mix thoroughly. Chill at least 30 minutes. Makes approximately ½ cup sauce

SWEET AND SOUR SAUCE

¾ cup tarragon vinegar
¾ cup brown sugar
½ cup water
1 ½ tablespoons soy sauce
½ teaspoon salt
¼ cup water
2 tablespoons cornstarch
¼ cup green pepper strips
¼ cup chopped green onions and tops
2 medium tomatoes cut into sixths

Combine vinegar, sugar, ½ cup water, soy sauce and salt. Bring to a boil and remove from heat. Combine ¼ cup water with cornstarch. Gradually add cornstarch paste to hot liquid, stirring constantly. Return to heat. Cook over moderate heat, stirring constantly, until mixture is thick and clear. Add green pepper and onion. Cook for 3 minutes. Add tomatoes. Serve over fried fish. Makes approximately 3 ½ cups sauce.

LEMON CAPER DRESSING

½ cup salad dressing (mayonnaise base)
1 teaspoon drained capers
1 tablespoon lemon juice
½ teaspoon prepared mustard
½ teaspoon Worcestershire sauce
2 drops liquid hot pepper sauce

Combine all ingredients. Chill. Makes approximately 2/3 cup salad dressing.

STONE CRAB MUSTARD SAUCE

½ cup sour cream
1½ tablespoons prepared mustard
2 teaspoons melted butter
½ teaspoon parsley flakes
1/8 teaspoon salt
Combine all ingredients. Heat at a very low temperature, just until warm, stirring occasionally. Do not boil. Makes approximately 2/3 cup sauce.

J. FOSTER'S BLUE CHEESE

1 cup mayonnaise, 1 cup good sour cream, 1 oz. white cooking sherry, ½ teaspoon garlic powder, 2 teaspoons celery seed, 1 6 oz. container of blue cheese crumbles (chopped). Stir and let sit.

DILL CRAB DIP

¾ pound blue crab claw meat, fresh or pasteurized
1 egg
¼ cup salad oil
2 tablespoons lemon juice
1¼ teaspoons dry mustard
½ teaspoon dried dill weed
½ teaspoon salt
Dash white pepper
½ cup salad oil

Remove any shell or cartilage from crabmeat. Place egg, ¼ cup salad oil, lemon juice, dry mustard, dill weed, salt and pepper in the blender. Cover and blend for 5 seconds on high speed. Continue blending on high speed while adding remaining ½ cup salad oil in a slow steady stream. Turn blender off occasionally and clean sides of the container. Remove mixture from blender container to a 1-quart bowl. Stir in crabmeat. Chill at least 1 hour. Makes approximately 2 ½ cups dip.
Variation: Use sesame or caraway seeds instead of dill weed.

KENT'S SCALLOP DRESSING

½ cup mayonnaise or salad dressing
2 tablespoons chili sauce
2 tablespoons chopped green onion and tops
2 tablespoons chopped green pepper
1 hard boiled egg, chopped
1 tablespoon chopped pimento-stuffed olives
½ teaspoon lemon juice
Dash salt and pepper

JUDY'S LOBSTER DIP

2 cooked lobsters, 1 avocado, ½ cup sour cream, 1 tablespoon mayonnaise, ½ teaspoon salt, ¼ cup grated onion, 6 drops tabasco, ½ teaspoon celery seeds.

Remove cooked meat from shells and cut into bite size pieces. Mash avocado. Blend with other ingredients except lobster. Chill and serve in a bowl surrounded by lobster meat. Makes 2 cups.

GREGORY'S SHRIMP CHEESE SPREAD

1 cup cooked shrimp, ½ pint cottage cheese, 2 tablespoons mayonnaise, 1 tablespoon prepared mustard, 1 tablespoon lime juice, 1 tablespoon tarragon vinegar. Salt to taste.

Chop shrimp. Mix cheese, mayonnaise, mustard, lime juice, vinegar and salt. Add shrimp. Sprinkle with parsley flakes and serve with crackers. Makes 2 ½ cups.

EASTPOINT CRAB PICKERS SPREAD

1-pound crabmeat, fresh or canned
1 package (6/10 ounce) Italian salad dressing mix
1 cup sour cream
½ cup mayonnaise or salad dressing
1 tablespoon horseradish mustard
Chopped parsley (garnish)
Assorted chips, crackers, raw vegetables

Remove any shell or cartilage from crabmeat. Combine crabmeat, salad dressing mix, sour cream, mayonnaise, and horseradish mustard; chill several hours. Garnish with parsley. Serve with crackers, chips or vegetables. Makes approximately 3 cups of spread.

OYSTER STUFFING

1 medium onion, minced
1 ½ cups celery, diced
1/3 cup butter
1 pint small oysters, drained and chopped
2 teaspoons mixed herbs
1 1/3 cup cooked rice
1 cup water chestnuts, chopped
salt and pepper

Cook onion and celery in butter until soft. Add remaining ingredients, mixing lightly. Makes 4 cups stuffing.

SCALLOP STUFFING (8-10 LB. BIRD)

1 medium onion, chopped
1 cup chopped celery
1 teaspoon leaf sage
1 teaspoon fish seasoning or savory
½ cup butter
1 loaf dry white bread (cubed)
2 cups scallops (chopped)
1 teaspoon salt
pepper

Sauté onions and celery with sage and fish seasonings in butter about 10 minutes. Add bread cubes, scallops, salt, pepper, mix well. Use 1 cup stuffing for each pound of turkey.

CREAMY SHRIMP SPREAD

½ pound cooked, peeled, de-veined shrimp, fresh or frozen
1 can (10 and ¾ ounces) condensed cream of mushroom soup, undiluted
1 package (8 ounces) cream cheese, softened
¼ cup ketchup
¼ cup finely chopped onion
Crackers or bread slices

Thaw shrimp if frozen. Chop shrimp. Combine soup, cream cheese, and ketchup in a 1 quart mixing bowl. Beat with an electric mixer until well blended. Add shrimp and onion. Mix well; cover and chill overnight. May be served on crackers or bread slices. Makes 3 ½ cups spread.

CHEESE GRITS

You may purchase Quaker® "instant" or buy a box and cook, following the serving size suggestions and cooking direction on the box. Some people prefer their grits plain, others with butter, or with cheese. I would suggest if adding cheese to your grits that you purchase a block of sharp cheddar cheese, grate it and mix into the grits before serving.
Another serving idea is to purchase old fashioned stone ground grits and cook them overnight in a crock pot. Add cheese before serving.

BASIC HUSHPUPPIES

1 cup cornmeal
2 teaspoons baking powder
½ teaspoon salt
1 egg
¼ cup milk
1 medium sized onion, minced

Mix dry ingredients and onion. Break in egg and mix well. Add liquid and shape into small patties. Fry at 375 degrees in deep fat, or in a skillet with about 1 inch of fat, until brown.

HEARTY HUSHPUPPIES

1 cup cornmeal
1 cup all-purpose flour
1 tablespoon baking powder
1 teaspoon sugar
1 teaspoon salt
1/8 teaspoon cayenne pepper
¾ cup milk or buttermilk (you can vary using milk, cream corn or beer)
2 eggs, beaten
½ cup chopped onion
¼ cup melted margarine or cooking oil

Sift dry ingredients together. Add remaining ingredients and stir only until well blended. Place a dollop of approximately 1 tablespoon of batter at a time into the hot oil. Fry until golden brown on both sides. Remove from oil and drain on paper towels. Serve. Makes approximately 4 dozen hushpuppies. Folklore has it that these tasty treats were created by hunters and fishermen from leftover batter and cooked to throw to their dogs to "hush the puppies"!

SWEET AND CREAMY COLESLAW

1 16 oz. bag coleslaw mix
2 tablespoons diced onions
2/3 cup creamy salad dressing
3 tablespoons vegetable oil
½ cup white sugar
1 tablespoon white vinegar
¼ teaspoon salt
½ teaspoon poppy seeds

Combine the slaw mix and onion in a large bowl. Whisk together the salad dressing, vegetable oil, sugar, vinegar, salt, and poppy seeds in a medium bowl; blend thoroughly. Pour dressing mixture over coleslaw mix and toss to coat. Chill at least 2 hours before serving.

TANGY COLESLAW

1 cabbage, finely shredded or a 16 oz. package of shredded coleslaw mix
1 medium red onion, quartered and thinly sliced
Dressing:
1 cup sugar
1 teaspoon salt
1 teaspoon dry mustard
1 teaspoon celery seed
1 cup vinegar
2/3 cup vegetable oil

Combine shredded cabbage with sliced onion
Combine dressing ingredients and bring to boil
Pour over cabbage and toss
Cool, then refrigerate
(This slaw is also great on barbeque sandwiches)

SWAMP CABBAGE (HEARTS OF PALM)

1 lb. ham bones r ¾ lb. ham hocks
1 can hearts of palm or 1 fresh cut swamp cabbage
Cook bones or hocks until done. Add hearts of palm. Salt and pepper to taste. Boil for 5 minutes.

SWAMP CABBAGE FAVORITE

1 medium onion, 2 slices bacon, 1 small can tomatoes, 1 can hearts of palm or 1 fresh cut swamp cabbage
Sauté bacon and onions. Drain most of liquid from hearts of palm. Add hearts of palm and tomatoes. Salt and pepper to taste.

FISH ROE WITH BACON

Separate three pairs of roe
Melt ½ pound butter or margarine in a skillet.
Roll roe in cornmeal seasoned with 1 teaspoon salt and ¼ teaspoon pepper.
Sauté slowly on all sides giving them time to cook through and until brown.
Remove and drain on paper towels.
Fry bacon crisp. Crumble and serve over top of roe.
Serves 4